CREATIVE DESIGN IN FURNITURE

WOOD, METAL, GLASS, AND PLASTICS

By WILLIAM H. VARNUM

Professor of Art Education, University of
Wisconsin, Author of "Industrial Arts
Design," "Pewter Design and Construction,"
"Commemorative Design"

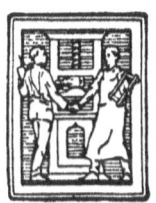

THE MANUAL ARTS PRESS

PEORIA, ILLINOIS

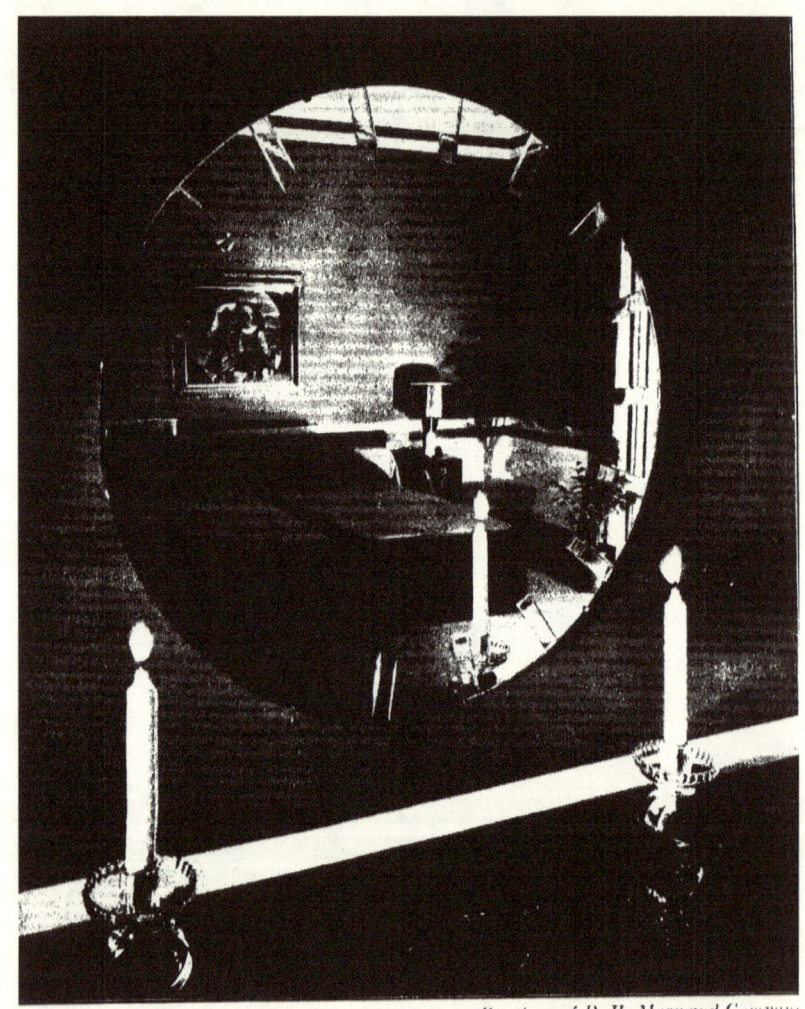

Simplicity and Space

PREFACE

IN a time of transitional development like the present, when period and modern furniture are intermingled in many homes and in most salesrooms, it seems opportune to examine the bases of contemporary furniture design. At such a time, it is especially appropriate to restate art principles, to point to their present applications, and to set forth the qualities of new materials coming into use in the construction of furniture. While many persons know some of the distinguishing characteristics of modern furniture, very few have an adequate appreciation of its significance; they have very little conception of the art movement that brought it forth.

With this viewpoint as a compelling motive in this book, an effort has been made to give lucid definitions of some of the new art terms. Widely divergent opinions exist as to exact meanings of some of these, but the author has attempted to bring together the most generally accepted definitions from both Europe and America. In some instances, it has been found necessary to set up new art definitions applicable to furniture design; but as nearly as possible these are in accord with modern practice.

Thus it is to be hoped that this pioneer book will so clarify modern designing as to make it a serviceable and enjoyable medium, both for the beginner and for the advanced craftsman and designer. While styles will change, the principles herein advocated are regarded as basically sound and so synchronized with modern architecture as to be thoroughly integrated with it, bringing furniture and architecture into harmonious relationship.

Functionalism, that activating agent of modernism, runs like a keynote throughout the book, and is detailed in Chapter One. Isometric rendering, modified to suit design requirements, is adopted as the vehicle for creative expression. It will be found amplified in Chapter Two.

Modern furniture design is considered as passing through three stages of development: (1) volumetric planning, (2) space-and-mass planning, and (3) the form stage. All points connected with the first stage are in Chapter Three; space-and-mass planning, the second stage, in Chapter Four; while the third, or form stage, is developed in Chapter Seven. The older and well-known art principles, such as balance, proportion, and rhythm, are introduced when they are needed for some specific purpose, and hence they occur in Chapters Three, Five, and Eleven. The theory of empathy is adopted in modified form and applied to clarify definitions of balance, rhythm, and thrusts.

Enrichment is introduced in the form stage and is of two types: plastic and surface. Enrichment brings with it knowledge of various types of plasticity and plastics, Chapter Six; while surface enrichment considers textures, veneers, and color, Chapters Eight, Nine, and Ten. Glass, metal, and bent wood and their design processes are detailed at appropriate points, together with some construction suggestions, although it is not the author's intention to write a construction handbook.

As the book progressed, the author considered it necessary to draw from the field of psychology a resumé of human desires and their relation to furniture design, curiously enough justifying many modern patterns through that source. These principles, finally applied to room planning and unit design, are found in Chapter Eleven.

In Chapter Twelve is developed what is believed to be a new approach to creative furniture design, based on functionalism, human needs, and beauty. At that point, the beginner, led through the technique of designing, is ready for the thrills of creative experience and its ultimate expression in creative construction.

If the industrial or manual-arts teacher is to keep abreast of the times, it becomes essential to advance his design knowledge. Likewise, the furniture salesman and interior designer must be familiar with the new terminology and its applications. Again, the new leisure brings with it the amateur craftsman who will naturally turn to the new forms and processes for his avocational development. To these, it is the author's hope to lead to new knowledge, to greater efficiency, to new vistas in creative art.

In order to keep the cost of the book as low as possible, and at the same time produce adequate illustrations, it was decided to omit expensive half-tone plates of photographs, and to use the line-cut process throughout. Simple and efficient beauty has been the objective in all illustrations within the delineating scope of the line-cut process, which in itself is expressive of the developments of this, the machine age.

Acknowledgment is extended to Gordon Hampel, a senior in the University of Wisconsin, for his faithful help in lettering and outlining many illustrations in the publication. The trade publication, *Creative Design*, has been a valuable source of contemporary information. Additional acknowledgment is extended to the Wisconsin Chair Company, Port Washington, and to their designer, R. G. Rideout, for permission to use motives shown in Figures 96 and 97; to Gilbert Rohde, designer of modern interiors, New York City, for privileges in relation to the bentwood chair designs on Plate 16; the Hekman Furniture Company of Grand Rapids, for Figure 98; the Johnson Handley Johnson Company also of Grand Rapids, for Figure 19; Popular Mechanics Magazine for courtesies extended in connection with illustrations of bending processes and the console table on Plate 15. Donald Deskey has contributed to our knowledge of glass design and construction.

From my files were selected several sketches without designation as to the designers. Modified to fit the text, some of these sketches have been used as illustrations; and it is the author's desire to extend due acknowledgment to these unidentified designers for their contributions in the field of creative design.

WILLIAM H. VARNUM

Madison, Wisconsin

CONTENTS

CHAPTER ONE
THE FUNCTIONAL SPIRIT
OF MODERN DESIGN

INTRODUCTION

IN recent years, a marked and growing interest in the field of design has spread through industry and education, while creative design is recognized as of vital educational merit and an avocational outlet for leisure. Recognition of design as an important part of the school curriculum, the growth of home workshops and hobby shows, the importance of beauty as an emphatic point in advertising literature and industry, indicate clearly contemporary trends in the art field.

A public, increasingly becoming conscious of good design, is further illustrated in an extensive questionnaire sent out by the Customer Research Staff of General Motors. In reply to this questionnaire, thousands of motorists voted *appearance* as more important than either speed or cost. It is valid reasoning to state that the presence of good taste and attractiveness in manufactured products is no longer a luxury, but a measuring stick of their desirability. It has been proved that an efficient product may be constructed perfectly, but, if poor in design, it will not sell.

Not only is the public demanding increased attractiveness in its purchases, with beauty bringing its sense of contentment, but it is becoming aware of the fact that much pleasure is derived by participation in the creation of beauty. This is particularly true with reference to designing things closely connected with home life.

For the craftsman, there is a very real pleasure in selecting wood or other materials and, with the tools of his craft, creating original designs in responsive and attractive materials. This process of constructive creation brings its own sense of completeness, of competence, of satisfaction, almost un-rivalled in its emotional results.

Many professional men, such as doctors, lawyers, clerks, and salesmen, have well-equipped workshops. They have come to realize that creative activity and construction afford a valuable emotional outlet for business troubles with complete relaxation. They bring to leisure time a profitable and restful *avocation* and *recreation*.

Copying designs of others is trying to shine by reflected light and is deadening in its mere display of tool technique. Copying a piece of furniture for the sake of its beauty is not essentially dishonest, provided the copy is as beautiful as the original, and provided it is neither intended for sale as a fake antique nor has been copyrighted. In this duplication, the craftsman is striving for the beauty of the original, but frequently the duplicate is only a feeble imitation of the original. In copying, the thrill of creative expression is entirely lost; while, educationally, it has little value and often turns out to be an unhappy experience.

From the foregoing paragraphs, the following points have been developed: (1) the increasing demand for better design by a public gradually becoming art-minded; (2) the self-satisfaction and value accruing from creative expression, particularly in the field of such intimate and useful products as furniture and its accessories; (3) the inadequacy of copied designs as a means of expression.

THE SPIRIT OF MODERN DESIGN AND FUNCTIONALISM

Commonly accepted trends point to a new type of design, currently known as modern or modernistic, but more appropriately called contemporary, as becoming increasingly popular. In 1929 the tide of older forms started to ebb, sweeping with it much of the Victorian, along with other types of furniture. The new style, the new tide, is bringing with it new plastics, new metals, new woods, and new processes with fascinating possibilities. The plush sofa is pushed out as a dust catcher, and, in many instances, modern furniture is replacing period designs. True, modern design is in a period of transition; styles of today may become the traditions of tomorrow, but the spirit back of the movement will remain. To understand this spirit, then, is of greatest importance to the designer. Consequently this book is predicated upon contemporary trends; but, in order to grasp their full significance, basic causes must be studied.

If we were to search for outstanding characteristics of the late nineteenth and twentieth centuries, they would be found in the growing interest in the natural sciences with their allied inventions and discoveries. In architecture, this interest has given rise to what is known as the theory of functionalism. The term "function" means the discharge or performance of any duty or emphasis on performance, in contrast with its form. For example, if the State capitol is built like a Renaissance structure, with emphasis upon its architectural form rather than its intended and functional use as a capitol of a state in the early and industrially efficient twentieth century, it is considered not as useful in its functional aspects as a modern building designed especially for the purpose of government.

Functionalism, with its axiom "Form follows Function," means that all modern architectural forms first must be determined by uses and environment, and that form must grow out of functions and construction. Le Corbusier, the Swiss-French architect, is quoted as demanding a function or use *for every detail of the house,* including, of course, its furniture.

For the extreme and radical believers in functionalism, the house becomes a machine emblematic of the machine age. Again quoting from Le Corbusier, "We no longer have money to build historical souvenirs. At the same time, we have to wash. Our engineers provide for these things and they will be our builders."

Thus strict observers of functionalism would give us a house planned by engineers for *comfort* in our home, *service* or a relief from the drudgery of unwelcome chores, and *freedom* from these by time-saving devices. Into this picture comes the electric refrigerator, oil and steam heating, dishwashers, air conditioning, and the numerous gadgets of this, our age of industry and mass production.

Under conditions now prevailing, these modern labor-saving devices are usually introduced into existing Colonial, Spanish, Georgian, or other traditional houses manifestly not adapted for the multiplicity of electrical outlets and other connections necessary for their installation—equipment unknown to former originators of these types. In other words, the house does not function as an integral part of its equipment.

To overcome this incongruity, we have arising a new type of house, often built of concrete, steel, glass; frequently prefabricated, which is the functionalists answer to modern conditions and new ways of living. In this house, there is plenty of space for sunlight and ventilation; flat, unenriched planes; glistening metallic surfaces, new materials, extreme simplicity and utility: all characteristics of the modern house—smoothly running and efficient machine of this age, embodiment of forms generated by the proper functioning of good living conditions and of the various appliances connected with living.

In these houses, beauty rests solely in proportioning, sculptural massing of parts, precise adjustments, and correct coloring. What type of furniture harmonizes with this house? Surely traditional design is questionable. Moreover, extreme functionalists are prone to question many things: the cellar with its waste of space, the use of moldings around the room (are paintings, then, nonfunctional?), the uses of small panes of glass, relics of times when large panes were too expensive for general use. And, of course, we see that extremists are against decoration which cannot be interpreted as contributing to use. Many houses of this character have been built abroad, but they hardly fit into American

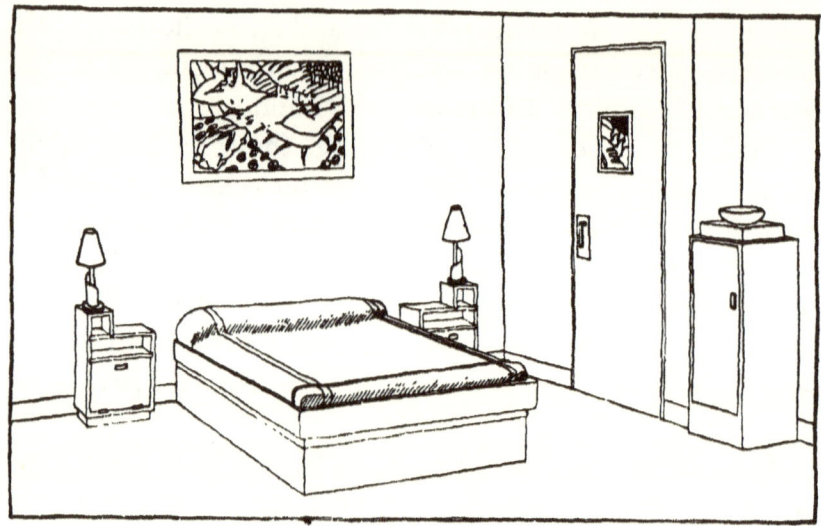

FIGURE 1.   Simplicity and Functionalism in Modern Design

ideals. In their over-plain, stark, almost factory-like masses, they fail to enshrine our ideals of home.

But the extreme functionalists and traditionalists are compromising; the functionalists introducing more beauty into their designs, while some traditionalists are relaxing the purity of the period forms. The influence of this is towards modifying design in the direction of greater beauty without strict questioning of its absolute utility. And so there are architects, while refusing to accept period furniture, who build, in the modern spirit, houses with a high degree of comfort, service, and freedom; but, with this difference: enrichment is permissible, provided it does not interfere with the structure of the house, is not artificial or "stuck on," and is in organic unity with the entire plan. The term "simple beauty and efficiency" may best interpret this latest development in both houses and furniture in its most modern aspects, of which Figure 1 and the frontispiece are expressive.

It may well be that the doctrine of functionalism eventually will do away with our present detached furniture in favor of the built-in type. The argument in favor of this is an improved appearance of the room and less chance for cluttered disorder.

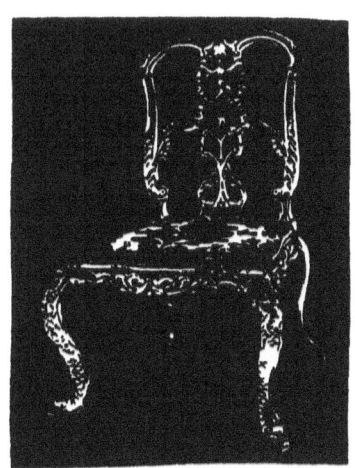

FIGURE 1a. Ornate Period Furniture

As few of us have purely functional houses, can we then make modern pieces of furniture and expect them to harmonize with existing conditions? Many people meet this condition by gradually replacing obsolete and functionless furniture with the more conservative of modern designs. Conservative functionalists still retain certain characteristics of period furniture, removing such meaningless curves and ornate decoration as are shown in Figure 1a, but with certain proportions and even curves intact. This is in no sense traditional furniture with a few modern touches added to it, a mongrel breed with characteristics of neither school of thought. The doctrine herein set forth and in which the author believes, does not concern itself with period or traditional forms; it considers either a reforming of period types, making all nearer functional, or adopting new forms based upon their functions in the affairs of life.

Two points may be noted regarding modern design: (1) Period furniture, representing as it does the lives and activities of ages differing from the present and with conditions far different, cannot be regarded as harmoniously planned for the modern house. Indeed, much period furniture illustrates the reverse of the axiom already discussed, "Form follows Function." Page 1 7. As a result of this condition, we have many homes from which furniture constantly is moving towards the repair shop or to the junk pile in the attic. Some of the period furniture has been cheap and poorly constructed, but much of it was broken because it was over-decorated and thus structurally weak. Functional forms of the modernist are intended to have a long span of service (too long, some manufacturers believe), and this purpose is built into their construction. (2) There may be a growing suspicion that the functional house with its furnishings lacks the charm and sentiment imparted by the older forms of furniture, rich with associations and memories. This is not necessarily true, for the functional house has its attractiveness in uses of beautiful materials, harmonious colors, comfort, space, and efficiency. It has its psychological and sentimental appeal, as we shall find, but of a different type from that assigned to the traditional.

After all is said, we are a people of differing tastes and standards; the home is the most conservative of our institutions and usually the last to respond to changing styles. At the present time, some individuals prefer period furniture— indeed, it may be in complete harmony with the lives of many; but, according to sales reports, the younger people seem to be moving in the direction of the modern.

CHAPTER TWO
TECHNIQUE AND TERMINOLOGY OF MODERN DESIGN

UNDER modern conditions, with emphasis on sunlight, plenty of air, and ventilation, *simplicity in design means a sufficiency of space.* Indeed, we shall find this question of space running like a keynote through modern design. This desire for space is also a reaction against the cluttered-up and stuffy house filled with meaningless bric-a-brac and ornate furniture: the chair upon which no one but a light-weight can sit; the rocker with its slender braces; the highly polished table, edged with cigarette burns; the painfully so-called comfortable chair; the tip-top table in name and deed; and so on. Along with these examples come the stuffily upholstered furniture which never seems to be thoroughly cleaned, with tidies protecting the upholstery from greasy heads.

A house and furniture should be so designed as *to welcome space.* Life should be lived in space, with its sunlight and air—space in architecture, in painting, in sculpture, in furniture, with its growing importance in the new design. Space leads to new methods of approach in designing and a new adjustment of prevailing terminology. While, as we shall see, certain art principles are age-old, and have always been true and important, there are three terms which assume new importance and whose interpretation must be understood. They are *volume, mass,* and *form,* structural and aesthetic steps through which the designer advances to the completed form.

VOLUME, MASS, AND FORM

Possibly the best method to understand clearly these terms
as applied to furniture design is through analogy with the
activities of the sculptor: Suppose, for instance, he is carving
a head and shoulders from the materials of his craft. First,
he selects a block of wood or stone, possibly rectangular in
its planistic relationship and just large enough to contain
his proposed conception. This block of material, we will call

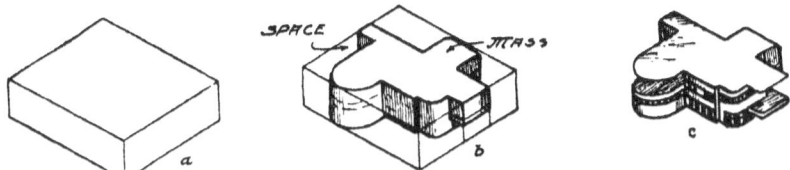

FIGURE 2.   *A*—Volumetric Casing; *B*—Mass and Space Stage;
C—Form Stage

his *volume.* As he drills his holes for depth, carves or chips
away his surplus material, he is creating a mass from the
volume of his stock; he has "roughed out" his design. We can
consider the outer surface of his original wood or stone block
a sort of casing or envelope, just enclosing the outside diameter of his pattern. As he continues to work on the
blocking-out process, he perfects the *mass* into that which we
will call its final *form.* The material chipped away forms
the *space* of his design. Thus the original block was the casing or *volume,* which went progressively through the
roughed-out or *mass stage* and the finished or *form stage.*

The space created by chipping away the material is an
important design element, and in modern treatment has considerable bearing upon appearances. Frequently, in designing rooms, interior space is augmented by the addition of
mirrors and glass which, by their reflections, give the illusion
of added space, as seen in the frontispiece.

From the viewpoint of advanced modern designers, space
is given a broader interpretation than the one adopted for

this text. In architecture, space is to be considered as extending indefinitely not only outside the volume, but the form itself must represent a complete interpenetration with outer space. "A dwelling should not be a retreat from space, but a life in space, in full relationship to it," says Maholy Nagy.

Thus, one can realize that modernists consider traditional architects as negligent in the full realization of space possibilities. In designing modern dwellings, some architects consider their designs first as volumes or bulks, subtracting space until they arrive at the mass of the design, often allowing space to penetrate entirely through the building for light and sunshine. This space may be enclosed by glass, but nevertheless it has the effect of space. In Figure 2, this plan has been depicted, in which *a* is the volume similar to the sculptor's block, *b* the roughing-out stage, and *c* the final or form stage, with light and air sweeping through the structure. New York sky lines seen through a

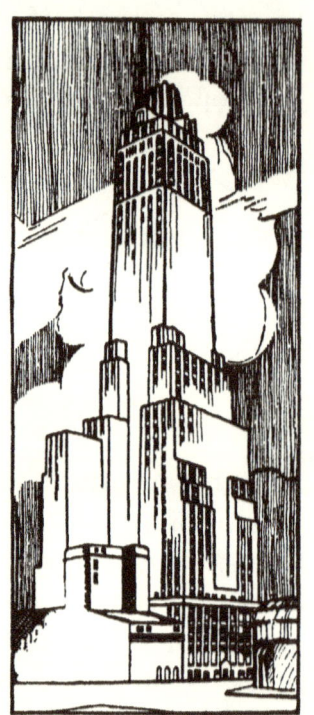

FIGURE 3.   The Form Stage

haze, and high buildings mistily obscured to blur form, give excellent impressions of architectural masses with spaces marking their outlines. Imagine Figure 3 under these conditions, and you will get the idea of the blocking-out stage quite clearly.

In period furniture, heavy designs, like Elizabethan and Jacobean, Figure 4, place emphasis on mass; lighter furniture, like Sheraton, for example, Figure 5, represents more space emphasis than mass; while, similarly, late Gothic

churches have impressive spaces and narrow masses. Gothic
architects appreciated light penetration; structurally considered, they did not have modern materials to aid them, with
the well-known results.

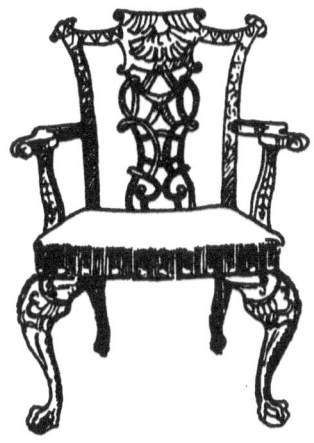

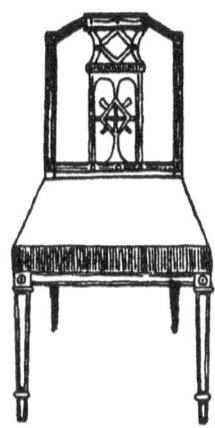

FIGURE 5. Space
Emphasis in
Period Fur-
niture

FIGURE 4. Mass Em-
phasis in Period
Furniture

THE VOLUMETRIC CASING OR ENVELOPE

Regardless of the amount of space and mass, the *volume*
from which these parts are subtracted is the starting point
of the design method advanced in this text. For furniture,
consider the volume as a transparent casing or box just enclosing the over-all dimensions of your design or piece of
furniture. For square or rectangular forms, Figure 6, the
volume must be rectilinear, while circular forms may also
be similarly planned. As will be increasingly clear, *the space
of the design is just as important as the mass of the design.*

What type of drawing is best adapted to the modern spirit,
and how can we delineate the factors of space and mass to
secure a comprehensive impression? Designing by means of
the customary side, front, and top views or, to use its technical designation, orthographic projection, is inadequate for

the purpose. In this type of drawing, each view shows but one side of the object, as front view, side view, and so on; and it is difficult to picture the whole design with its spaces and masses in their positions and in complete relations—to assemble these views in the mind as a picture of the whole pattern.

The term "picture" in the previous paragraph suggests the use of perspective, showing simultaneously several sides and thus allowing one to compare masses and spaces. The major objection to this method is this: To design in perspective, one must be a capable perspective draftsman, with complete knowledge of the subject—the result of training which few beginners possess. Moreover, it is desirable in some way to measure one's sketch, and perspective measurements are indeed difficult.

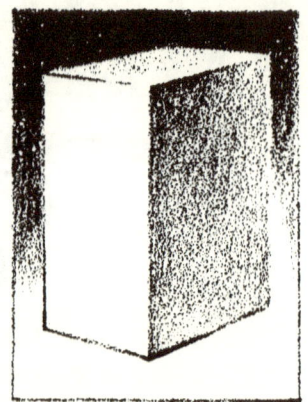

FIGURE 6. A Rectilinear Volume

MODIFIED ISOMETRIC

These objections are partly answered by the use of what will be termed "modified isometric," illustrated on Plate 1 and explained in the following paragraphs. If isometric drawing may be termed "conventionalized perspective," modified isometric can as readily be called "stylized perspective." And, as modern design is extensively stylized, modified isometric drawing seems eminently satisfactory as a design vehicle for creative expression.

Without entering into details, let us say that isometric projection in its unmodified form is based on representing a cube, placed in such a manner as to cause the rear, lower corner to be exactly covered by the front, upper corner. This view is developed by tipping the cube, as shown in

Figure 7, Plate 1, through several positions until *a,* Figure 7, gives the basis for isometric projection.

Figure 8, Plate 1, shows the cube of Figure 7 turned around in usable form. It is noted that all receding horizontal edges are at an angle of thirty degrees to a horizontal line and, while three surfaces are shown, there are no vanishing points.

The lack of convergence in retreating edges, but always seen in actually looking at objects, gives a "pushed-up" appearance to the rear surfaces, particularly of long objects, also the illusion of a slight increase in height in vertical planes as they go back from the front, vertical edges. However, as one becomes accustomed to the views, these defects and distortions no longer become troublesome.

Moreover, in isometric practice, it is customary to measure actual lengths, widths, and heights directly on the cube or other form, as shown in Figure 8, Plate 1. For vertical edges and heights, this practice is not open to objection; but measuring surfaces which retreat or go back from the front make them appear too long.

These objections are met by the following procedure: The 30° angle of isometric has been retained as a feature, and the volumetric casing of rectilinear objects is drawn as is the cube of Figure 8. All *heights may be measured directly on vertical lines* wherever they may occur and in the appropriate scale, as will be developed in this chapter.

Shortening all retreating surfaces to simulate their actual appearances, or foreshortening, brings us to the use of a new drawing instrument, the foreshortening triangle.

THE FORESHORTENING TRIANGLE

The *foreshortening triangle* can be made from the tip of an old 30°–60° triangle by sawing and filing and finally finishing with sandpaper. The full-size drawing of this triangle is shown in Figure 7a, and is exactly the size with which the drawings in this book were made. A heavy sheet of celluloid

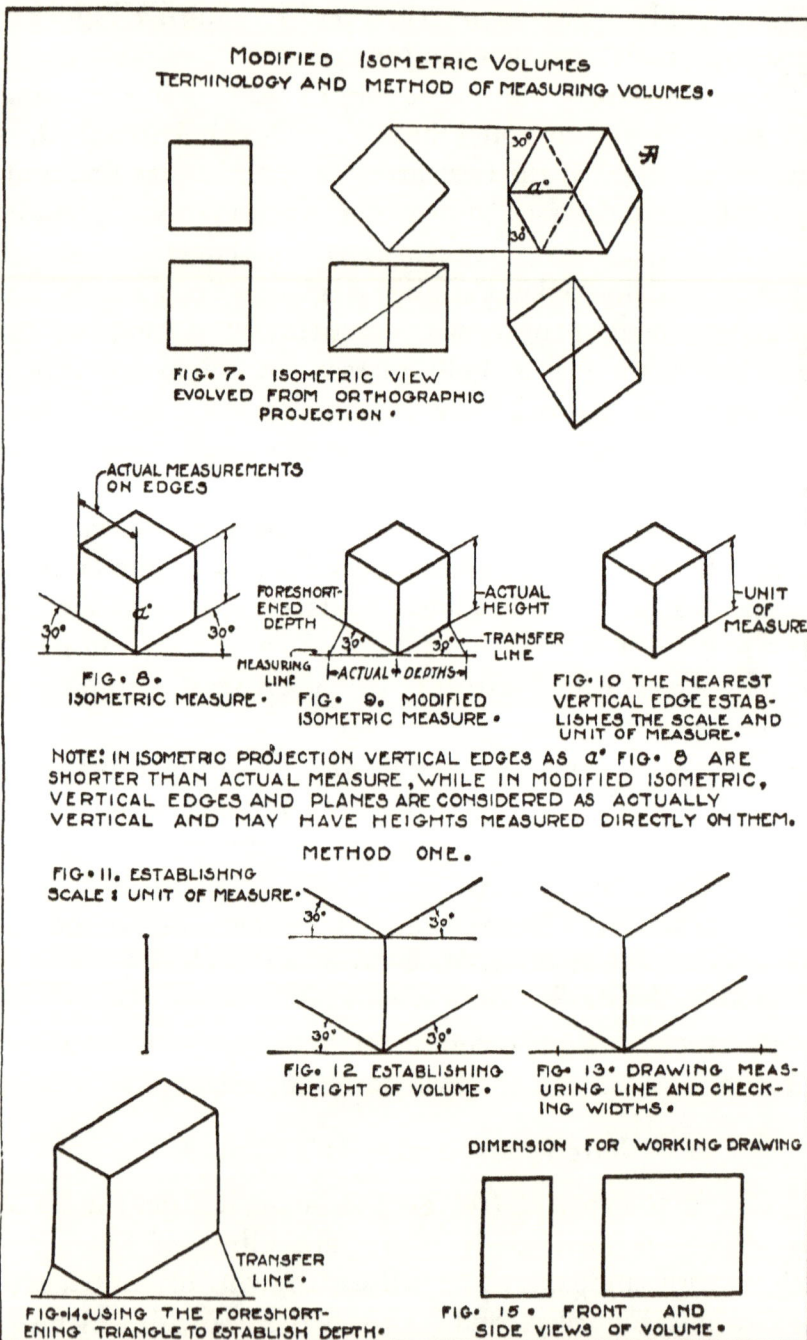

MODIFIED ISOMETRIC VOLUMES
TERMINOLOGY AND METHOD OF MEASURING VOLUMES.

FIG. 7. ISOMETRIC VIEW
EVOLVED FROM ORTHOGRAPHIC
PROJECTION.

ACTUAL MEASUREMENTS
ON EDGES

FIG. 8.
ISOMETRIC MEASURE.

FORESHORT-
ENED
DEPTH

MEASURING
LINE — ACTUAL DEPTHS

ACTUAL
HEIGHT

TRANSFER
LINE

FIG. 9. MODIFIED
ISOMETRIC MEASURE.

UNIT
OF
MEASURE

FIG. 10 THE NEAREST
VERTICAL EDGE ESTAB-
LISHES THE SCALE AND
UNIT OF MEASURE.

NOTE: IN ISOMETRIC PROJECTION VERTICAL EDGES AS $a°$ FIG. 8 ARE
SHORTER THAN ACTUAL MEASURE, WHILE IN MODIFIED ISOMETRIC,
VERTICAL EDGES AND PLANES ARE CONSIDERED AS ACTUALLY
VERTICAL AND MAY HAVE HEIGHTS MEASURED DIRECTLY ON THEM.

METHOD ONE.

FIG. 11. ESTABLISHING
SCALE & UNIT OF MEASURE.

FIG. 12 ESTABLISHING
HEIGHT OF VOLUME.

FIG. 13. DRAWING MEAS-
URING LINE AND CHECK-
ING WIDTHS.

DIMENSION FOR WORKING DRAWING

TRANSFER
LINE.

FIG. 14. USING THE FORESHORT-
ENING TRIANGLE TO ESTABLISH DEPTH.

FIG. 15. FRONT AND
SIDE VIEWS OF VOLUME.

Plate 1

of the approximate thickness of a triangle serves adequately. It is possible to use thick, tough cardboard, as supplied with this book.

In use, the actual depth of the volume is measured on the horizontal line, as in Figure 9, Plate 1. This line is termed the *line of measure*. The transfer line, made with the long edge of the transfer or foreshortening triangle, carries this distance properly foreshortened to the surface to be measured, and registers the depth of the surface. By studying Plate 1, these points of procedure will be clear, particularly in Figures 8 and 9. Heights are measured as in true isometric. Compare the cubes of Figures 8 and 9 for the improved and more natural appearance of the modified form.

There are still objections and distortions in the method, but in time, the experienced draftsman will make allowance for these; while the type of procedure itself is the simplest and least technical for the purpose of creative design. Moreover, the completed modified isometric sketch is *capable of being measured* and translated into the working drawing from which the design is constructed.

The designer should have both the 30°, the 60°, and the foreshortening triangles at hand for immediate use, using the latter only for measuring. If desirable, this triangle may be reinforced with a firmer cardboard backing.

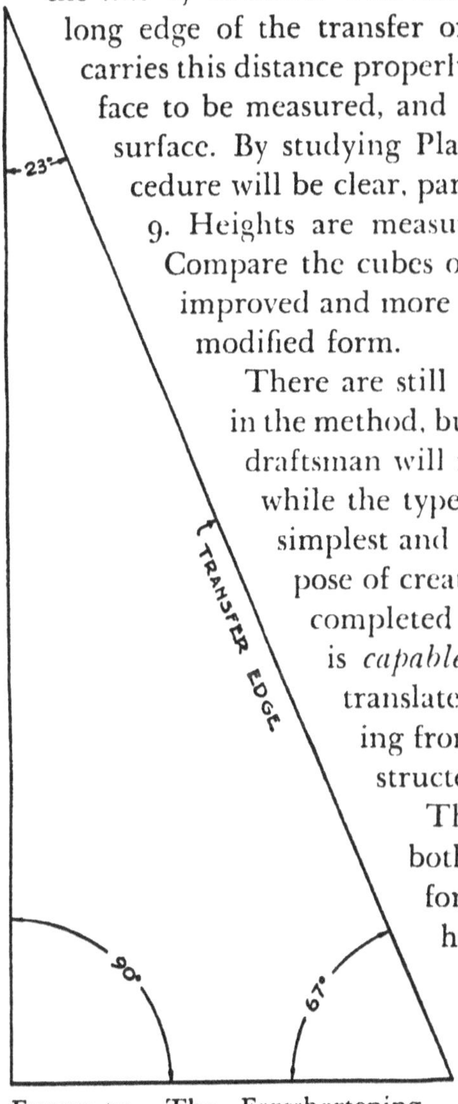

FIGURE 7a.   The   Foreshortening Triangle

THE VOLUME AND ITS ISOMETRIC RENDERING
Method One

To become thoroughly familiar with this new technique, the beginning designer should pursue the step-by-step procedure which follows. Let it be assumed that the dimensions of the volumetric casing are known.

Step 1. It is customary to select some scale for the design. Frequently, the scale of one and one-half inches to the foot is serviceable, while larger objects may be reduced to one inch to the foot. Small objects are to be drawn full size. For the coming study of proportioning, the metric system is invaluable as a timesaver and, if one so desires, the scale of one millimeter to equal one centimeter is adequate.

Step 2. For convenience, the nearest vertical edge of the volumetric casing is always drawn first and designated as the unit of measure, Figure 10, Plate 1. Figure 11, Plate 1, establishes this edge drawn to the selected scale with the 30° triangle and T-square, as is the customary practice in instrumental drawing.

Step 3. From the top and base of the unit of measure, extend light lines indefinitely to the right and left with the 30° triangle, thus defining the height of the volume, Figure 12, Plate 1.

Step 4. Draw a horizontal line through the base of the vertical edge or unit of measure of the volumetric casing indefinitely to the left and right. This is the line of measure. From the front corner, where that corner touches the line just drawn, measure the widths or depths of the left and right surfaces, using the scale originally selected. This step completed appears in Figure 13.

Step 5. With the long edge of the foreshortening triangle on the T-square, transfer these true lengths to their foreshortened or apparent lengths by means of the transfer lines, as in Figure 14, Plate 1.

Step 6. Complete the volume, as shown in Figure 14. To avoid interference with the lines of the volume, *all transfer lines must be kept light.*

The volume now stands complete, with three visible surfaces showing in their approximate relationships and sizes. Spaces and masses readily may be planned within this volume, with an approach to reality and the advantages of this technical approach quickly appreciated.

Step 7. Figure 15 depicts Figure 14 translated into the customary working drawing for shop production, minus, of course, its dimensions.

THE CREATIVE APPROACH TO VOLUME DESIGN
Method Two

Designing is a creative process by which we express our feelings, our emotions, regarding art forms. Let us consider some specific problem as, for example, a coffee stand. For creative designing, there must still be established a unit of measure, as so many inches to the foot, large enough to give freedom to our design attempts.

Step 1. A slightly different method of handling the unit of measure is preferred by some designers. With T-square and triangle, draw the center edge of the volume which later will enclose the coffee stand, Figure 16, Plate 2. Select some convenient unit of measure for the front edge, as 100 millimeters or one inch to the foot, and measure off on the front vertical edge, as at Figure 16, Plate 2.

Step 2. With the 30° triangle, extend the edges of the volume, as at Figure 17, Plate 2, to the left and right.

Step 3. Check off on these edges what you feel to be the correct and pleasing widths for the sides, keeping the lines free and light.

Step 4. Complete sides and top. Study all planes of the volume; left, right, and top. Do the surfaces seem too nearly alike or monotonous? Do you feel that they could be im-

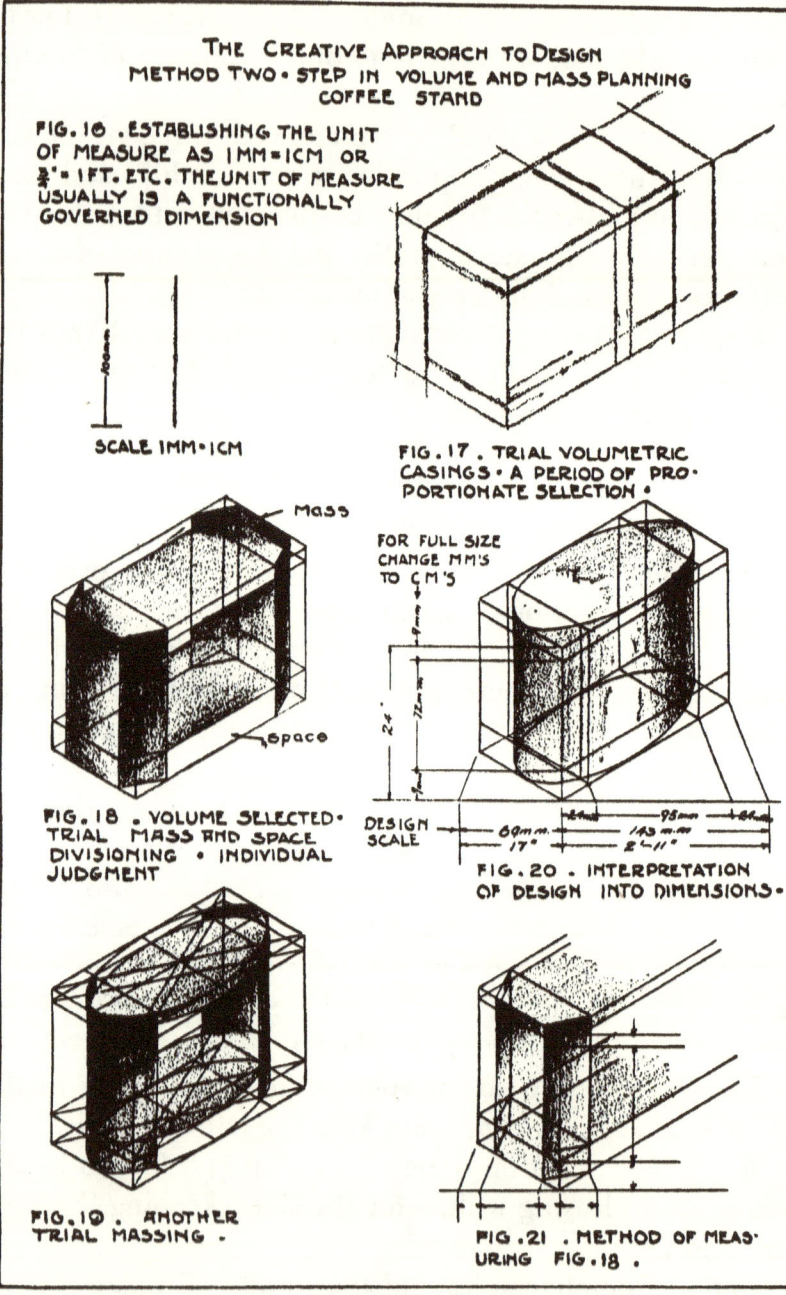

THE CREATIVE APPROACH TO DESIGN
METHOD TWO • STEP IN VOLUME AND MASS PLANNING
COFFEE STAND

FIG. 16 . ESTABLISHING THE UNIT
OF MEASURE AS 1MM=1CM OR
¾"=1FT. ETC. THE UNIT OF MEASURE
USUALLY IS A FUNCTIONALLY
GOVERNED DIMENSION

SCALE 1MM•1CM

FIG. 17 . TRIAL VOLUMETRIC
CASINGS • A PERIOD OF PRO-
PORTIONATE SELECTION •

Mass

Space

FIG. 18 . VOLUME SELECTED•
TRIAL MASS AND SPACE
DIVISIONING • INDIVIDUAL
JUDGMENT

FOR FULL SIZE
CHANGE MM'S
TO CM'S

DESIGN
SCALE

FIG. 20 . INTERPRETATION
OF DESIGN INTO DIMENSIONS•

FIG. 19 . ANOTHER
TRIAL MASSING .

FIG. 21 . METHOD OF MEAS-
URING FIG. 18 .

Plate 2

proved by making them more varied? It is well to try several proportions until a satisfactory volume is established. This volume is to indicate the character of your stand, and too much care cannot be given to this fundamental process. Draw in the selected volume and erase all trial lines. This now stands as your creative effort.

Step 5. Check the volume for its functions. Will the stand be steady and stable and serve its purpose as to sizes?

Step 6. Draw the mass and space divisions and develop several designs. Figures 18 and 19, Plate 2.

Step 7. Form, the final step, is left for later consideration. Keep all masses and spaces varied. Note that your feeling, your sensitivity to proportioning of spaces and masses, is given full opportunity of expression.

Step 8. All thought in the preceding steps is given to *creative effort* plus function as a control. At this point reverse the steps of Method One. By transfer lines and foreshortening triangle, carry the volumetric and other depths to the line of measure by the foreshortening triangle and the transfer lines and, selecting the scale approaching the desired size, record the dimensions and proceed to check them for functional and proportionate reasons, as will be developed in the next chapter. Many variations of Methods One and Two will occur to the designer, particularly as he increases in knowledge. Note Figures 20 and 21 for measuring devices.

The following chapters will consider in detail various aspects of modern design as it affects the volumetric casing and its space and mass divisions.

CHAPTER THREE
VOLUMES: THEIR PROPORTIONS AND QUALITIES

SIGNIFICANT LINES

CONTEMPORARY designers use lines for their emotional qualities, their ability to sway our emotions being partly through their innate qualities and partly through associations grouped around them. In creating new forms and reshaping the old, *line significance*, its character and spirit and how it influences us, must enter into the problem.

Much has been written as to the significance of the horizontal line so popular with modernists. Modern automobile design has emphasized the long, horizontal line, usually unbroken from end to end, as a symbol of speed in transportation. In architecture, the horizontal lines, as seen in structural steel, floors, steps, and so on, are expressive or significant of stability and rest. Our bodies in repose assume a horizontal position. Summarizing these facts, we can truly say that the unbroken horizontal, or a broken line giving the impression of the horizontal, stands for repose and stability plus energy and vitality; it is a positive, straightforward, reliable type of line, and this is its usual significance to most of us.

Modern designers have used the horizontal in every imaginable way, with its appearance in furniture integrated with its appearance through repetition in draperies, rugs, and other accessories, as in Figure 143, page 141, and constantly referred to in this text. It is a line of marked utility and beauty, fitting well into this age which requires both vitality and reliability; but, with changing trends, other lines shortly may become predominant. Indeed, certain dealers seem to sense the decline of the horizontal as now under way.

Vertical lines, as in trees, columns, the human figure in an erect position, have more vigor than the horizontals, greater lightness, and a feeling of growth and support. As horizontals

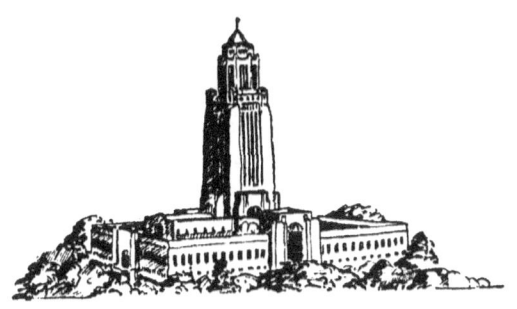

FIGURE 22.   Significant of Power and
Activity

and verticals bound most of the volumetric casings used in this book, it is logical to believe that *verticals and horizontals appearing as bounding lines generate similar feelings;* but *either one or the other must dominate* or we will be trying to say two things, particularly if each type of line has equal significance. We must either say it with verticals or with horizontals, or the results will be confusing and the message conveyed by the lines lost in confusion.

It will be found that beauty and interest in volumes will consist of two things: the *significance of the type of line* we use, its associations; and the *beauty of proportionate relationships* existing in the volume.

DYNAMIC AND STATIC VOLUMES IN RELATION TO LINES

Volumes are divided into two classes, the *dynamic* and the *static*. The term dynamic is defined as relating to the effect of forces or moving agencies in nature. Thus a dynamic form (if it is to be considered as beautiful) must have significance, a sense of movement, of life and activity.

The antonym of the term "dynamic" is "static," connoting a state of complete rest and immobility. A typical static form is the cube. With its equally balanced verticals and horizontals, it has no significance and has no message for us. Let us then avoid its use as a volumetric mass or volume. It is characterless and lifeless.

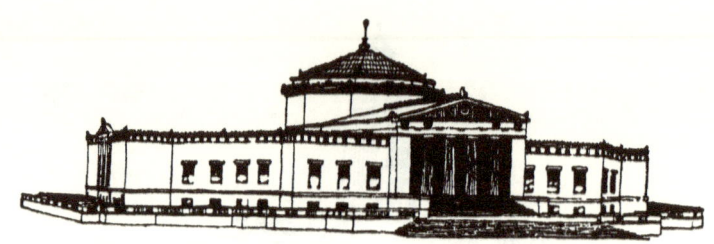

FIGURE 23.   Significant of Security and Stability

But as we shall see, a clever designer may introduce the static square (one of the cube's faces) in a lively volume, and its very restful, lifeless, static qualities become elements of beauty. Used alone, however, the cube is considered of poor proportions and not beautiful.

The towering volume of Figure 3 gives a sense of power, activity, and elation, for the vertical line in its full significance dominates the volume. In Figure 22, a combined vertical and horizontal theme, but with the vertical dominant, is honest, straight-forward, solid, individual, but with dynamic traits and power.

Contrast these volumes with the dominantly horizontal volume of Figure 23. The horizontals are not sufficiently unbroken for much indication of speed, but there is security and permanence.

Thus, by controlling the height, width, and depth relations clearly enough, we are in direct control of the impressions received by others. For the sake of brevity, let us call a volume that is higher than it is wide, a vertical volume, with all the significance found in lines of that nature, Figure 24; while a volume, like Figure 25, is a horizontal volume,

with its spaces and masses delivering a strong, lateral push
or thrust. For clarity, the volumetric casing is omitted.

As an additional illustration of this point, a chair designed
for comfort and rest could not well be designed as a vertical
volume—its significance would be incorrect; while a chair
for temporary use, as for dining purposes, is essentially a
vertical volume, conducive to lively, vital conversation, to

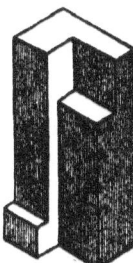

FIGURE 24.
Vertical
Volume
with Up-
ward
Thrust.
Casing
omitted

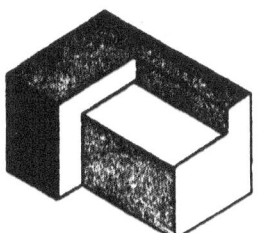

FIGURE 25.   Horizon-
tal Volume with Lat-
eral Thrust.
Casing omitted

a feeling of well-being and strength. This question of function and the type of correct volumetric proportioning is
almost an intellectual study, but line and volume significance has passed the experimental stage and must be counted
as an established fact.

But, besides giving the volume its significance through the
emotional and associative appeal to accord with its intended
function, there is the question of beauty of its proportions;
for, unless the volumetric envelope has this beauty, the bene-
fit of significant line will be lost. Indeed, it may well be
claimed that a volume both with functional significance and
beauty of proportioning has the richest and fullest possible
significance.

Proportions and Linear Relationships

Beauty in proportioning plays an important, almost a major, rôle in modern furniture design. Modern design has been defined as simple in appearance, with much of its charm resting in the finest of proportionate relationships.

Proportion means comparative relationships of one thing to another. Applying this to volume, it refers to the relationship of all sides to each other and all spaces and masses within the volume. Proportioning even goes a step beyond the volume; it includes the integration of the volume with the remaining volumes in the room, a point developed under Unit Planning in Chapter Eleven, page 131.

Linear Relationships

Proportionate relationships may be expressed either by geometric or arithmetical terminology. For example, suppose we say of a line, "It is one inch long." We cannot judge its proportions, for there is nothing with which it can be compared; but, by placing near it another line two inches

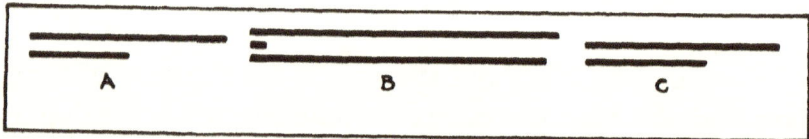

Figure 26.   Linear Relations

long, as in Figure 26, *A*, there has been established a basis of comparison. *Ratio* (meaning the relationship or proportion of one thing to another) of these lines is expressed arithmetically as 1 to 2; while two lines 150 and 300 millimeters long respectively or any other pairs of comparable length, would be expressed by the same ratio.

But what are the characteristics by which these good proportions to which we have referred are judged? Study the lines of Figure 26, *A*, for subtlety and variety. Variety means

intermixture or succession of different things, while subtlety
refers to delicately adjusted and refined relations. Is there
anything indicating delicate adjustment in two lines, one of
which is twice as long as the other? The answer is obvious:
the proportionate relationships between these lines is lacking in subtlety and variety; or, in other words, they are
monotonous.

Now compare the relationships between the lines of Figure 26, *B*, and apply the same tests. Easily we determine the
fact that there is too much variety and little delicacy. Compare *B* and *C*, Figure 26. Which have the better proportionate relationships? Usually any relationship easily solved by
eye measurement alone is disliked as lacking in subtlety and
variety, as is the case of the 1 to 2 ratio.

The static square has no subtlety and variety, and yet modern designers have found for it occasional use, particularly
to reduce the activity of a lively design, and to produce a
resting point.

The ratios so far considered are termed "linear," referring
as they do to line relationships. A rule-of-thumb method of
checking subtlety is to divide the length of the lesser line into
that of the greater. If the quotient is a whole number, as
$300 \div 75 = 4$, the relationship is pretty sure to be unsatisfactory. A quotient of $1.61+$ is one of the very best ratios we
have. If the quotient is near a whole number, as 3.02 or 1.98,
the proportionate relationship is characterless and indefinite
and lacks decision, while incommensurate quotients are to
be preferred to commensurate figures.

PROPORTIONATE AREAS

Linear proportions are comparatively simple to judge, particularly if one is sensitive to the aesthetic qualities in these
matters. With practice, ability to judge planes and volumes
will become easier. Look at the two rectangles of Figure 27.
Which do you prefer? Which is more dynamic?

While the relationships of planes as well as lines may be expressed by arithmetical terms, as 5 to 8, the relation of width to height, or the static 1 to 1, it is becoming common practice to let one term stand for a particular plane or area. This term is determined by dividing the lesser dimension of the plane into the greater. An example of this would be a plane measuring 100 millimeters by 100 millimeters: the quotient is one and this then always stands for a square.

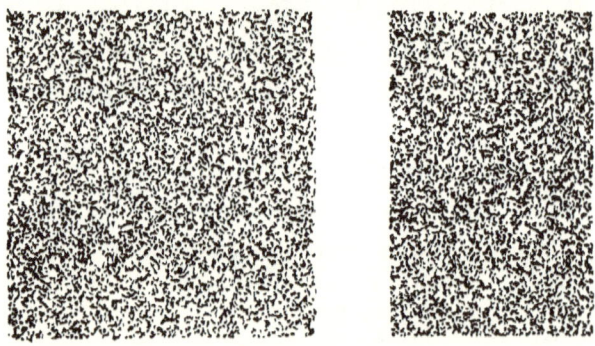

FIGURE 27.   Judgment of Proportionate Areas

An area measuring 100 millimeters by 150 millimeters or 1.5 would be a square and a half, with proportions of 1 and 1.5, indicating little subtlety or variety and consequently not pleasing as interpretations of beautiful proportions.

Contrasting with these proportions are two areas measuring 100 millimeters by 141+ millimeters, or an area of 100 millimeters by 161.8 millimeters. The ratios of both are respectively 1.41+ and 1.618, both ratios expressing extreme subtlety and beauty with no equal divisions of the square in them, as can be seen in Figure 27a. Compare these areas with the square of Figure 27. While these examples have been illustrated by the metric system (by far the simplest system for studying proportionate relationships), tests may be applied equally well to feet and inches by reducing fractions of inches to decimals. Thus, an area measuring three

and one-eighth inches by six and five-eighths inches has a
ratio of 2.12+.

As in this text we are dealing with creative expression,
it is best to use your own taste in planning proportions, as
shown in Method Two, page 32, and then checking results
by the arithmetical process suggested in the preceding paragraphs. It is true, however, that many individuals do not
have a fine sense of discrimination in proportionate relationships, or are in need of intensive training leading to

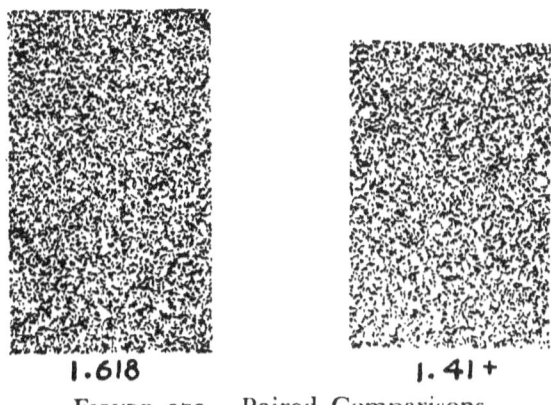

1.618   1.41+

FIGURE 27a.   Paired Comparisons

acute judgment. For these individuals, the following sections have been inserted.

JUSTIFICATION FOR A SYSTEMATIC PROPORTIONATE APPROACH

Further justification for the following approach to proportioning rests in the strong, aesthetic appeal found in
arithmetical and geometric factors. Running through
modern and Greek design, one discovers a distinct system
of orderly proportioning by which pleasing and beautiful
results are possible.

In many epochs, poets and philosophers have referred to
the orderly beauty of geometric patterns; while the summa-

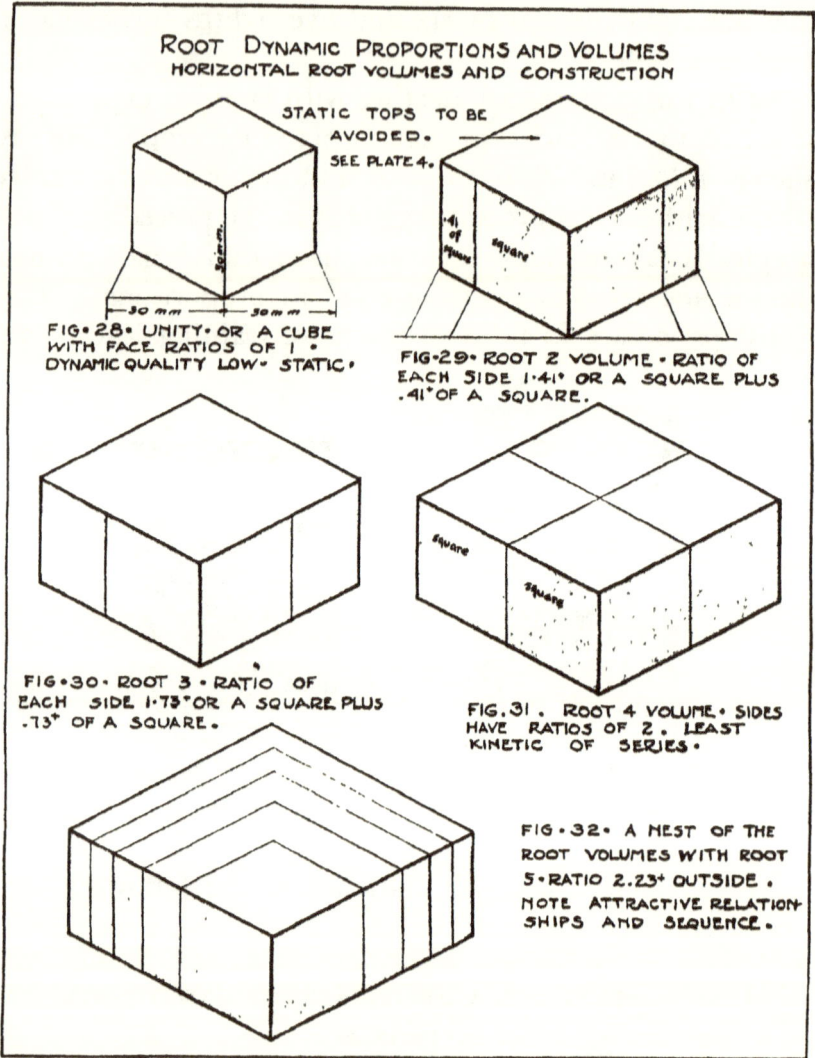

ROOT DYNAMIC PROPORTIONS AND VOLUMES
HORIZONTAL ROOT VOLUMES AND CONSTRUCTION

STATIC TOPS TO BE
AVOIDED.
SEE PLATE 4.

FIG.28. UNITY. OR A CUBE
WITH FACE RATIOS OF 1.
DYNAMIC QUALITY LOW. STATIC.

FIG.29. ROOT 2 VOLUME. RATIO OF
EACH SIDE 1.41* OR A SQUARE PLUS
.41*OF A SQUARE.

FIG.30. ROOT 3. RATIO OF
EACH SIDE 1.73*OR A SQUARE PLUS
.73* OF A SQUARE.

FIG.31. ROOT 4 VOLUME. SIDES
HAVE RATIOS OF 2. LEAST
KINETIC OF SERIES.

FIG.32. A NEST OF THE
ROOT VOLUMES WITH ROOT
5. RATIO 2.23* OUTSIDE.
NOTE ATTRACTIVE RELATION-
SHIPS AND SEQUENCE.

Plate 3

tion series of numbers, 3-5-8-13-21- and so on, each number representing the sum of the two preceding numbers, is the basis for the ionic curve or the spiral, Figure 138, page 133, the most attractive of all curves. Well-known arithmeticians assert that beauty in proportioning may be reduced to a mathematical basis, while designers claim that the beauty in modern design rests mainly in its proportions. These points are potent reasons for the following approach, with the distinct reservation that any mathematical theory is a good servant but a poor master; while a sensitivity to proportioning frees one from all forms of mathematical or geometrical approaches.

THE HAMBIDGE RECTANGLES

Through many years of careful research in the design methods of the early Greeks and Egyptians, Jay Hambidge, among other discoveries, found a large number of Greek vase forms which fitted exactly in certain rectangles—rectangles which possessed interesting relations to each other. Five of these rectangles are outstanding and are of value to us as representing dynamic areas used by the best of all proportionists, the Greeks.

Full explanation of the Hambidge theory is not adapted to the objectives of this text; consequently, ratios alone are considered. Omitting the square with its ratio of 1, the parent rectangles rediscovered by Mr. Hambidge are termed the Root Two Rectangle, with its ratio of 1.41+, shown volumetrically in Figure 29, Plate 3; the Root Three Rectangle, with a ratio of 1.73+, Figure 30, Plate 3; the Root Four Rectangle, with a ratio of 2, Figure 31 (this seems to be the least satisfactory of the series); the Root Five Rectangle, with its ratio of 2.23+, Figure 32, Plate 3; and the Whirling Square Rectangle, or XM Rectangle, with a ratio of 1.618+, Figure 27a. For comparative purposes and excepting the whirling square, these rectangles have been assembled into

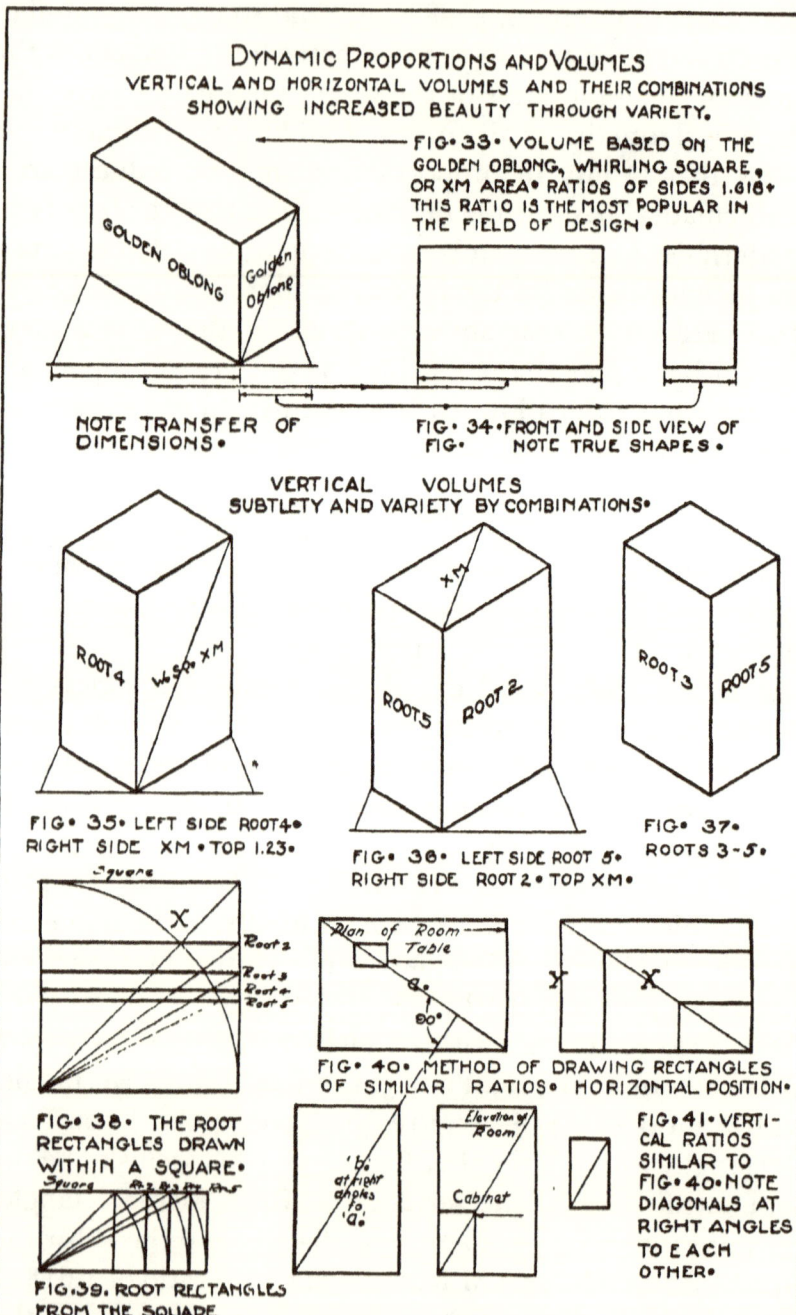

DYNAMIC PROPORTIONS AND VOLUMES
VERTICAL AND HORIZONTAL VOLUMES AND THEIR COMBINATIONS
SHOWING INCREASED BEAUTY THROUGH VARIETY.

FIG· 33· VOLUME BASED ON THE
GOLDEN OBLONG, WHIRLING SQUARE,
OR XM AREA· RATIOS OF SIDES 1.618·
THIS RATIO IS THE MOST POPULAR IN
THE FIELD OF DESIGN·

GOLDEN OBLONG — Golden Oblong

NOTE TRANSFER OF
DIMENSIONS·

FIG· 34·FRONT AND SIDE VIEW OF
FIG· NOTE TRUE SHAPES·

VERTICAL VOLUMES
SUBTLETY AND VARIETY BY COMBINATIONS·

ROOT4   Wb SQ· XM

FIG· 35· LEFT SIDE ROOT4·
RIGHT SIDE XM ·TOP 1.23·

XM
ROOT5   ROOT 2

FIG· 36· LEFT SIDE ROOT 5·
RIGHT SIDE ROOT 2· TOP XM·

ROOT 3   ROOTS

FIG· 37·
ROOTS 3-5·

Square
X
Root 2
Root 3
Root 4
Root 5

FIG· 38· THE ROOT
RECTANGLES DRAWN
WITHIN A SQUARE·

Square

FIG· 39· ROOT RECTANGLES
FROM THE SQUARE

Plan of Room —
Table

a
90°

FIG· 40· METHOD OF DRAWING RECTANGLES
OF SIMILAR RATIOS· HORIZONTAL POSITION·

'b·
at right
angles
to
'a.'

Elevation of
Room

Cabinet

Y   X

FIG· 41·VERTI-
CAL RATIOS
SIMILAR TO
FIG·40·NOTE
DIAGONALS AT
RIGHT ANGLES
TO EACH
OTHER·

Plate 4

volumetric casings on Plate 3, while their relations to each other are depicted in Figure 32, Plate 3. Grouped as they are in Figure 32, their wonderfully rhythmic relationships are shown to advantage.

Plate 4 was drawn to illustrate fully these rectangles in various volumetric combinations through which their beauty of rhythmic proportionship, their vigorous character, and strong dynamic qualities may be appreciated and so justify Mr. Hambidge's designation of "Dynamic Rectangles." For illustrative purposes, the tops of all volumes on Plate 3 were drawn as squares, while on Plate 4, as this is no longer necessary, much variety is shown by the various combinations.

The dynamic rectangles can be constructed readily by means of the metric scale. If 100 millimeters has been adopted as the unit of measure for the front edge of the volume, multiply 100 by the desired ratio, as 100x1.73, the Root Three ratio. The result, 173, is the desired length of the side, and 173 millimeters may be measured, as in Method One, page 31. For convenience, the metric scale is appended, while a small celluloid scale is available for a few cents.

10 millimeters equal one centimeter

10 centimeters equal one decimeter

10 decimeters equal one meter

Obviously all pieces of furniture cannot be designed within the volumes based upon various combinations of Root Rectangles, as indicated in Figures 33 to 37 on Plate 4. But, at any rate, practice in drawing these rectangles will lead towards better understanding of proportionate relations.

You will observe that Figures 35, 36, and 37 on Plate 4 are *vertical volumes,* composed of variously proportioned Hambidge rectangles. For these vertical volumes, select a unit of measure as 50 or 100 millimeters, and multiply it by the desired ratio as follows: For Root 2— .705, Root 3— .576, Root 4— .5, Root 5— .447, and, for the Whirling Square, .618. Lay the result off on the line of measure, project to the desired edge, and the proportion has been completed. Example: It is desired to make one face of the volumetric casting a Root Three ratio in a vertical position. Select a unit of measure as 100 mm. and multiply by .576. The product, 57.6 mm., is then measured off on the line of measure and checked up by familiar procedure with the foreshortening triangle. Horizontal ratios and volumes are formed by multiplying the unit of measure by the ratios referred to in the opening paragraphs of this section.

For those individuals who prefer the geometric approach to Root Rectangle construction, reference is directed to Figure 38, Plate 4, in which the Root Rectangles are drawn within the square. The construction and geometric processes are self-evident. In Figure 39, the Root Rectangles have been drawn in order outside the square and again, in their juxtaposed positions, their rhythmic relationships are revealed.

SIMILAR RECTANGLES

This chapter cannot well be closed without reference to that useful device for repeating similar rectangles; that is, rectangles of exactly similar ratios. Thus, by duplicating similar forms, we have produced harmonious beauty through repetition. These similarly proportioned rectangles may be either larger or smaller than the parent form.

For an example of similar rectangles, note the 1.618 ratios of Figures 33, 35, and 36, Plate 4. You will observe that their diagonals are all parallel, regardless of their varying sizes. Referring to the right-hand drawing of Figure 40, Plate 4, you can readily understand the method of creating a number of rectangles of varying sizes but of similar ratios, drawing any desired line far enough to intersect the diagonal *x* of the rectangle *y*, which gives the corner of a new and similar rectangle.

The left-hand figure of 40 shows the plan of a room and the diagonal method of proportioning the table to repeat the room ratio, giving unity through similarity. To make a rectangle of exactly the same proportions as the room plan of Figure 40, construct the line *b*, Figure 41, at right angles to the line *a*, the room diagonal. By constructing a rectangle based on the diagonal, as shown, one can create furniture elevations of exactly the same ratios as found in the room plan.

Application of this scheme is seen in Figure 41, in which a cabinet has one side harmonizing in its ratio with the room plan of Figure 40 and the wall elevation as well. Naturally these are almost ideal conditions, but repetitions of similar ratios wherever possible are desirable moves in the direction of integrating ratios throughout the room into harmonious and unified proportionate beauty.

CHAPTER FOUR
THE SPACE AND MASS OR BLOCKING-OUT STAGE

AFTER a necessarily thorough treatment of volume and its proportioning, the second step in furniture design is reached: the planning of mass and space within the volume.

Briefly, as has been stated, this is the "blocking-out" period in which the functional parts, as shelving, seats, drawers, table tops, clock faces, and other *structural features*, are allotted their respective areas within the volume. Small details of construction, as thicknesses of shelves, are to be left until the form stage is reached. The main thought in mind now is to keep details out of the way until the large mass and space areas are attractively proportioned and arranged. The plan is to move from the *whole* to its *parts*.

ORDER

Whether we consider ancient, period, or modern design, there are age-old principles which must control massing and spacing. The foremost principle is that of order, nature's leading law. Poor design, ugliness, discord are conducive to actual bodily discomfort; often mental restlessness and nervousness are the results of discordant sounds and atrocious color.

Disorderly and discordant furniture is a clear indication of mental and physical slackness and uneasiness. As the constant repetition of irritating sounds will cause discomfort, so constant observation of chaotic conditions, furniture in disorderly array, will produce similar irritation and "get on the nerves."

This condition is out of step with modern design, which seeks to give relief from these conditions and administer to our comfort through simplicity and beauty. The correction for disorder is orderly thinking, orderly habits, furniture designed with some orderly systematic plan. Thus a littered desk may be reassembled into order, a crowd adjusted into orderly lines, and an intricate furniture design brought into a readily comprehended whole by orderly mass and space planning.

The number of separate spaces and masses in a design registers its degree of complexity. The measure of success of an object depends upon the success with which complexity has been brought into an orderly arrangement. To remember this, think of the formula for artistic value: Artistic meas-

$$\text{ure} = \frac{\text{Order}}{\text{Complexity}}$$

There are a large number of degrees of complexity in furniture, varying from the intricate Chinese Chippendale to the medium degree of complexity found in the William and Mary, and finally to the simplest, the modern. Directly correlated with complexity is construction; complicated designs are much more difficult to construct adequately and keep serviceable.

THE FIELD

First, there must be selected from the field some specific volume so planned as to function perfectly for its designated duty. This field has rich possibilities, many of them outside the home, each element in the field having its own characteristics and functions. These characteristics must reflect such close gradations as articles designed for family life, personal privacy, seclusion for study, domestic comfort coupled with social contacts, social service, business contacts, judicial dignity, recreation, professional life, athletics, and many others.

Each field has its properly proportioned volumes, spaces, and masses which may be determined by its specific functions supported by the emotional and associative line aspects connected with and impregnating the problem. For example, furniture for a business office or a schoolroom would not have the same volumetric relationships as a piece designed for domestic comfort. It is up to the designer to analyze the situation.

When the volume has been designed, its space and mass divisioning calls for equally careful consideration, for the more space removed from the volume, the lighter the piece of furniture and the more different the associations aroused by its lightness and by the effect of lightness on serviceability. Should chairs designed for business contacts be as light as chairs designed for social contacts?

In the past, the question usually was this, "Shall I use a William and Mary, a Chippendale, or a Sheraton pattern?" The modernist asks, "What type of form is best adapted for this particular service?" and then goes ahead and creates his new forms, which may not, in any way, bear relations to past forms.

STEPS FOR SPACE AND MASS PATTERNING

To clarify space and mass procedure, let us take some problem selected from the "family life" group.

Specifications: A cabinet for toys containing one open shelf and nine drawers. Let us suppose we are moderate functionalists and, while the cabinet must be fully serviceable, it must contain beauty for the child's environment. As a safeguard against upsetting and for the significant values in the volume, the cabinet is to be horizontal in spirit.

As functionalism is a constantly recurring theme, a strong, tough wood should be selected; and, to increase the functional possibilities of this design, let us decide that the chest or cabinet is for his playthings and is to contain drawers, each of a different color to guide him in putting away his toys in systematic order, a toy for each color. By these colors, the child will learn to look for his belongings, at the same time increasing his color knowledge. Thus the specifications are continued until all possible service is extracted from the problem.

Step 1. Take a sheet of white drawing paper, reasonably smooth and capable of standing erasing, and fasten to a drawing board with adhesive (Scotch) tape at the corners. Locating the head of the T square on the left edge of the drawing board and placing the 30°-60° triangle on the top edge of the T square, we are ready to begin the design. Hereafter, follow either Method One or Two as suggested. Pages 31, 32.

In selecting the dimensions for the volume, height is the first consideration. A good plan is to have of equal height all available furniture in the child's room, partly for plenty of light and ventilation through the absence of unduly high furniture cutting off the summer's breezes, and partly for its unifying effect, giving to many articles of furniture in the room a common denominator in a common height. The device of the common denominator is a distinct aid towards establishing desirable order in the complex situation created by many pieces in the room. Let us establish a full-size height of 76 centimeters or approximately 29⅞ inches.

With a sharp HB pencil, draw the front corner of the volume as shown in Figure 42, Plate 5. For drawing this line, select some scale for the unit of measure which will be easy to handle on the drawing board and large enough for details. A convenient scale for a design of this size is 1 millimeter to 1 centimeter. Proceed to check off 76 millimeters on the line you have just drawn.

Step 2. Draw a light, horizontal line (the line of measure) through the lower end of the vertical line, Figure 42. If the unit plan is followed, as explained in Chapter Eleven, we must make the left side of the cabinet the same depth as other

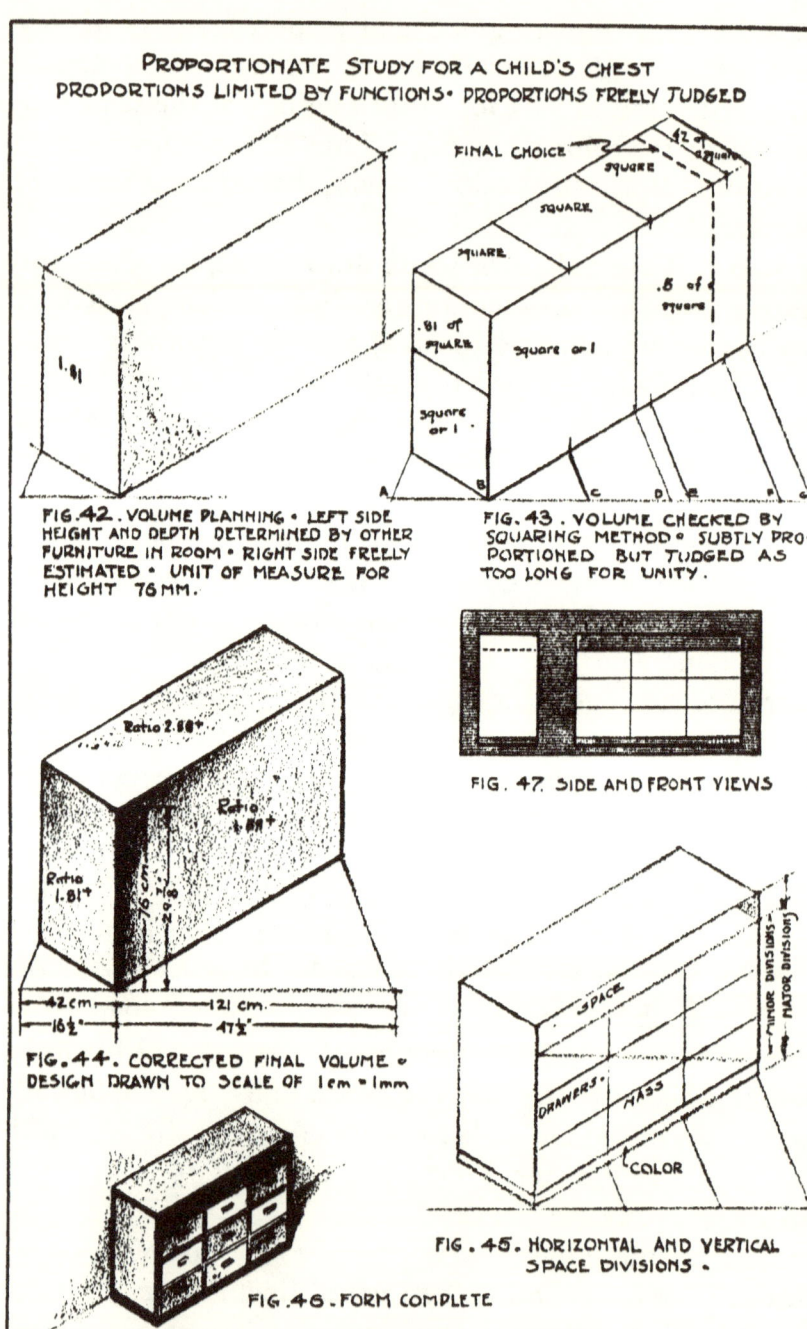

PROPORTIONATE STUDY FOR A CHILD'S CHEST
PROPORTIONS LIMITED BY FUNCTIONS • PROPORTIONS FREELY JUDGED

FINAL CHOICE

FIG.42. VOLUME PLANNING • LEFT SIDE HEIGHT AND DEPTH DETERMINED BY OTHER FURNITURE IN ROOM • RIGHT SIDE FREELY ESTIMATED • UNIT OF MEASURE FOR HEIGHT 76 MM.

FIG.43. VOLUME CHECKED BY SQUARING METHOD • SUBTLY PRO-PORTIONED BUT JUDGED AS TOO LONG FOR UNITY.

FIG. 47. SIDE AND FRONT VIEWS

FIG.44. CORRECTED FINAL VOLUME • DESIGN DRAWN TO SCALE OF 1cm = 1mm

FIG.45. HORIZONTAL AND VERTICAL SPACE DIVISIONS •

FIG.46. FORM COMPLETE

Plate 5

articles in the room and of similar nature. For example, if
other tables or chests in the room are 42 centimeters deep,
the left side of the chest must conform. Let us, then, adopt
42 centimeters as a hypothetical depth. With the foreshortening triangle placed on the top edge of the T square and
following the procedure of Method One, page 31, create the
left side of the volume, which should measure 76 by 42
centimeters full size, or 76 by 42 millimeters reduced size.
If you so desire, check the ratio at once by dividing the
lesser dimension into the greater. You will see that the quotient is 1.81, satisfying the requirements for proportionate
variety and subtlety.

Step 3. By your eye, and following Method Two, page 32,
check off a length for the right side, using your sense of proportioning and judgment regarding lengths for the drawers,
although the exact planning of the latter need not be clearly
seen at this phase of volume planning.

In Figure 42, Plate 5, the lines of the volume have been
completed and our impression is this: The right side evi-
dently is too long for a unified volume. In other words, the
volume is "stretched out" so far that the attention does not
comprehend the right, left, and top sides as one volume.

Even in this overlong condition, it is interesting to check
the sides by arithmetical methods, and, for this purpose, the
volume has been redrawn in Figure 43. By bringing the
volume down to the line of measure by our foreshortening
triangle, we can measure the sides, preferably by the metric
system as a timesaver.

The front vertical is arbitrarily established at 76 millimeters, the left side is 42 millimeters wide, and the right
side is 143.6 millimeters. Summarized and reduced to their
ratios, they present the following:

Left Side 76x42 mm........Ratio 1.81
Right Side 76x143.6 mm....Ratio 1.81
Top Side 42x143.6 mm....Ratio 3.42

By the squaring or geometric method of checking, it is seen that the left side is composed of a square plus .81 of a square, for the square always counts as one, or unity. By measuring the height on the line of measure, *BD*, and transferring the dimension to the right vertical side, we note one square plus .81 of a square, exactly similar to the left side and proved both by the arithmetical and geometrical methods. By checking off the width of the left side on the line of measure, Figure 43, as *BC*, *CE*, *EF*, and carrying the lines to the top, it is found to consist of three squares and .42 of the fourth square.

Analyzing the situation, this is where the cause of dissatisfaction rests: In a large piece of furniture, horizontal in character, and with drawers which will make the volume seem longer, it is advisable to shorten the volume. The attention may be held to a tall, vertical mass; but, in horizontal masses, the attention is apt to move away from the volume, and the volume loses our complete attention and so suffers in aesthetic value. Later on we shall find various devices, like grouping and thrusts, to aid in holding attention; but, with present knowledge, the volume will be shortened.

By trial and error, several volumes are sketched until one, labelled "Final Choice," Figure 43, and, for illustrative purposes, redrawn in Figure 44, is selected, which, if desirable, may be analyzed as follows:

> Left Side 42x76 mm.......Ratio 1.81
> Right Side 76x121 mm......Ratio 1.59
> Top 42x121 mm..........Ratio 2.88

If it is more convenient to translate these dimensions into feet and inches, a quick and approximately correct method is to secure a meter stick with inches on the reverse side, and, remembering the scale of one mm. equals one cm., locate the measurement in centimeters and, by reversing the stick, read the dimension in feet and inches, with the following results:

Left Side   29⅞″x16½″....Ratio 1.81
Right Side 29⅞″x47½″....Ratio 1.59
Top   47½″x16½″....Ratio 2.87+

Step 4. In this step, Figure 45, we are introduced to the system for orderly space and mass planning, namely by space and mass divisions, shown in the form of light lines traversing and cutting the volume in varied proportionate divisions but related to it. In modern design, these divisions have structural justifications and add to the feeling significance of the volume.

First sketch in the major divisions as the shelf and the bottom color band. Naturally the shelf functions better at

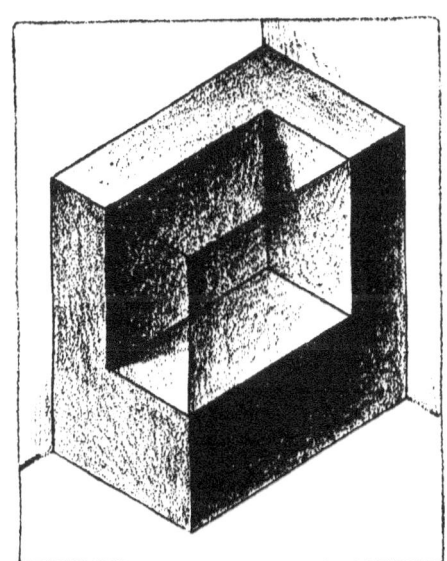

FIGURE 48.   Major Space and Mass Plans for a Child's Cabinet

the top and is so located. Check the mass to be filled with drawers *as a whole or unit.* Compared with the shelf and color band, are the results monotonous or are the spacings equal? Are certain major divisions too small for the others? These points are matters with which your sensitivity to mass and space adjustment has to deal.

Step 5. The drawers represent minor divisions in this increasingly complex situation which must be brought into order. For the child's convenience in replacing them, the drawers will be made the same size; although educationally there may be an advantage in varying their sizes and so letting the child make some specific drawer fit into its proper place.

And so, while the drawers are to be equal in size, we can make them proportionately related to the mass which is to contain them. Note the diagonal of Figure 45 and the obvious and familiar method by which the nine drawers are similarly proportioned to each other and to the central major division. For similar proportions, refer to Figure 40, Plate 4.

This step completes the space and mass pattern with the shelf occupying *space*, while the band and drawers represent *mass*. At this point, we are not concerned with the final appearance of the chest as these factors enter into the

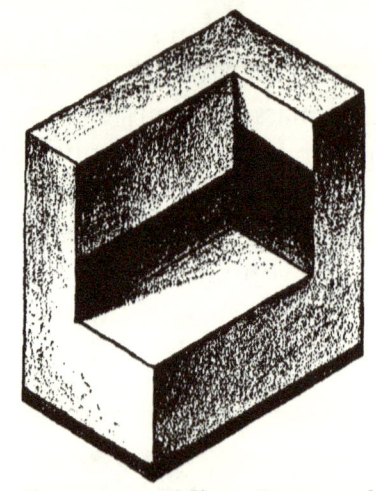

FIGURE 49.   Minor Space and Mass Plan for Child's Cabinet

Form Stage of progress; but, for satisfaction associated with knowing what the final result will resemble, we have appended Figures 46 and 47, modified isometric, with side and front views of the finished project.

A variation of this design is illustrated in Figure 48. In this pattern, space has been removed from the volume to form a ledge or shelf for toys, with the major divisions shown in Figure 48. In Figure 49, the minor divisions are indicated, locating such structural parts as additional shelf space, lockers and possible drawer space, all constituting minor mass and space divisions based on the space and mass main or major divisions of Figure 48. Note the proportioning problems in the proper allocation of all working or functioning parts. For convenience in converting fractions to decimals and millimeters to inches, see pages 154, 155.

CHAPTER FIVE
B A L A N C E

WHILE in Chapter Four we studied the technique and the functional logic back of space and mass patterning, there are other ageless design principles which must be known to the designer to guide him in his space and mass planning. The modern significance of these principles is just as important today as in the times of the Egyptians.

As emphasized in Chapter Four, space and mass divisioning lines form a pattern of interlacing lines crossing the volumetric casing, mapping the different surfaces into smaller areas. While in Chapter Four emphasis was placed on the *structural significance* of the divisions, nevertheless we added a major division, a color band, at the base of the child's cabinet, as in Figure 46. This band had little structural use excepting as a scuffle band, hence it must have been added to improve the *appearance of the design*, which points out that space and mass divisions, while primarily structural, may have an aesthetic function, thus placing a broader construction on functionalism. We are beginning to suspect that the term function may mean more than to be purely serviceable. We are beginning to accept the fact *that beauty in an article may have a distinct functional bearing upon our well-being,* and *hence be of service.*

This brings us to a consideration of the eternal principle of balance, checking, as it does, both stability and beauty. For furniture designers, there are four forms or types of balance: (1) balance of spaces and masses, (2) balance of thrusts, (3) balance of tone, (4) balance of color. What are their effects in furniture design?

DEFINITION OF BALANCE

Balance means holding all parts of the design together in equilibrium. "Is the design top-heavy? is it one-sided? is it unstable?"—all, usually, queries regarding balance. Figure 52, Plate 6, is emblematic.

Lack of balance will cause us to feel uncomfortable, with a desire to move our bodies in such a manner as to restore balance. Subconsciously we actually restore balance in our bodies or suffer the results in a fall. Subconsciously we do the same form of correcting when we see an unbalanced design.

The vaudeville performer who piles tables and chairs to form a tower, climbs to the top and rocks the column backward and forward, is an example of unbalance. We, in turn, subconsciously rock our bodies in a direction which will check his fall, trying to restore his balance. Foot- and basketball games call forth much of our mass response to this stimulus.

It is believed that this physiological response has a distinct connection with our desire for proper balance. A perfectly balanced pattern will give a feeling of ease and rest with an appreciation of the pleasure accompanying this phase of beauty successfully accomplished.

SPACE-AND-MASS BALANCE PATTERNS

While the foregoing explanation deals with balance as a general problem, we must now deal with specific balancing phases in current practice. The most common form of space-and-mass balance is illustrated in Figure 50, Plate 6, and is identified as *formal* or *symmetrical balance*. Even masses on each side and of equal volume balance on the space in the center of the desk. In other words, it is like-sided balance, and Figure 55, Plate 6, is of a similar type of pattern.

Like most design principles, analogies may be found in

BALANCE AND PLASTICITY
COMMON TYPES

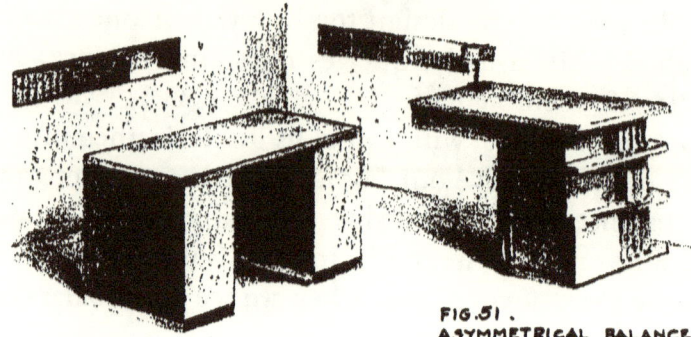

FIG. 51.
ASYMMETRICAL BALANCE

FIG. 50.
SYMMETRICAL BALANCE

PLASTIC TYPES OF
MASSES AND SPACES

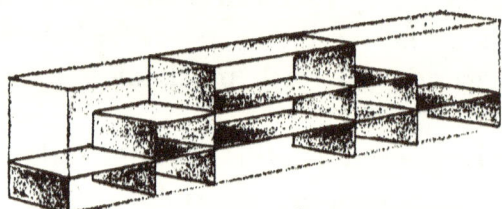

FIG. 55. PIERCED AND
AND PENETRATED TYPE.
WINDOW STAND.

FIG. 52. LACK
OF BALANCE

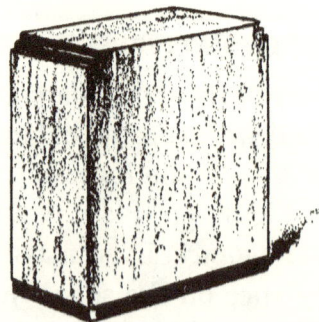

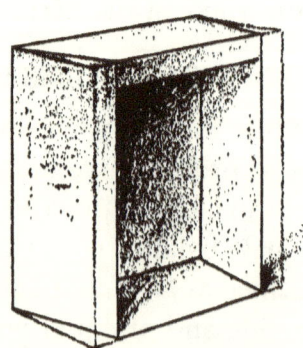

FIG. 53. MODERATELY PENETRATED
TYPE. CLOCK CASE.

FIG. 54. DEEP PENETRATION.
SPACE AND MASS FOR DESK.

Plate 6

the human anatomy. Seen from the front, we are sym-
metrically planned, although there are minor variations in
the shapes of shoulders, ears, and so on. Similar variations of
a minor nature are permissible and even desirable in furniture design. In the desk of Figure 50, articles placed on
the desk top vary the purely symmetrical plan.

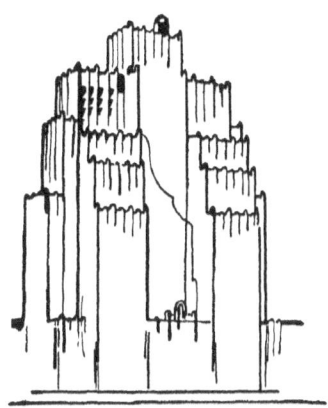

FIGURE 56. Symmetrical
Balance in Architecture

Thus any type of design whose
controlling or principal face
shows equal left and right distribution is referred to as being in
symmetrical balance. While the
desk in Figure 50, Plate 6, is of a
simple pattern, Figure 56, an architectural example, shows much
more complexity; yet it is symmetrical. Analyzed, Figure 56,
with more space removed from
the volume than is the case with
Figure 50, is an example of the
well-known set-back architectural feature; while its mass
pattern shows rhythmic progression or sequence, but with
more variety than developed by the arithmetical 3-5-8-13-
progression of the summation series. Viewed from the front,
the pattern is nearly symmetrical. Figure 51, Plate 6, represents a far more difficult type of mass-and-space patterning
which is termed *asymmetrical balance,* an antonym for symmetry, in which the masses are not placed in like-sided balance but nevertheless are planned to give us a feeling of
equilibrium. If you bend your body out of balance, you restore balance by projecting another part of the body until
equipoise is restored; the greater distance you push an arm
or foot from the body, the greater is its power to restore
balance.

In Figure 51, Plate 6, the heavy mass in its center is the
body. On one side the top is projected out and, to balance

this extreme distance, three short shelves on the left complete the equilibrium. Three shelves form a rhythmic progression which is one of the most pleasing contributions to proportionate relationships.

There are no definite rules for either symmetrical or asymmetrical balance; it is a matter of feeling. While symmetrical balance is easier to control in pattern, many designers prefer asymmetry. This may be due to the sedate, dignified, and stable characteristics of symmetry compared with the active, restless moving qualities of asymmetrical planning; but each type has its logical place in the room.

Mass-and-Space Proportions

Not only must masses be balanced, but their proportions must be carefully considered. Under no conditions is it good taste to remove from the volume equal parts of space and mass. The sum of all spaces removed from the volume must not equal the sum of all the masses. Then, unless demanded by strict functional requirements, do not have many spaces and masses of equal sizes, or nearly equal, which is as unattractive.

By correct proportioning, keep the spaces and masses from appearing clumsy. Necessary complex details frequently may be grouped together as were the drawers in the child's cabinet, and thus count as one mass. Check all parts of your design for oversmall or overlarge masses which seem to be out of scale with other parts. Out-of-scale masses and spaces cut up the design and so destroy its essential organic unity.

Thrust Balance

In Chapter Three, the significant meaning of lines and volumes was found to be of marked importance in *modern designing*. Spaces and masses have thrusts or movements of equal significance, which, if incorrectly handled, will not

only destroy the significance of the mass, but will give the
illusion of distortion to the entire design.

By referring to the description of balance in the first part
of this chapter, we find that the unbalanced vaudeville performer apparently was aided by our body thrusts. In a foot-
ball game, almost subconsciously, we push with our team
against the opponents, not only to restore balance, but to
give a dominant thrust or push to our team, to shove it across
the scoring line. On the other hand, there is a feeling of dissatisfaction if the thrusts of the home team meet with little
opposition. We seem to thrive on thrust combat.

By an interesting series of parallels, our subconscious
mental attitudes about the game illustrate our aesthetic feeling about design thrusts. These thrusts bring to design a
freedom and freshness, life and action; but the thrusts must
be *controlled* and *balanced effectively* or the stability of the
design will be upset. Yet one thrust feeling must run through
space and mass, usually similar to the horizontal or vertical
character of the volume.

As explanatory of thrusts, we refer to Figure 58a, in which
both vertical masses and minor details give a decided up-

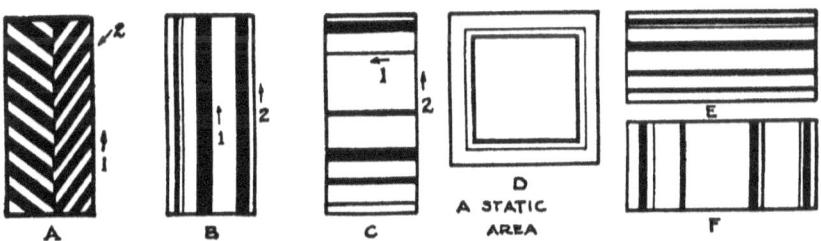

FIGURE 57.   Diagrammatic Thrust Patterns and Their
Relations to Structure

ward thrust and pattern to the design, balanced nicely by
the restraining horizontals.

In Figure 57 are space and mass divisions arranged in
various patterns. In *A,* we feel two dynamic thrusts at work,

the enclosing vertical rectangle, *1*, giving to the pattern its upward thrust, while the slanting lines, *2*, give opposing inward and downward thrusts. What is the effect? The slanting thrusts are so powerful that the top of the rectangle appears narrower than the base, although it is actually the same width, thus creating distortion disastrous to the structure

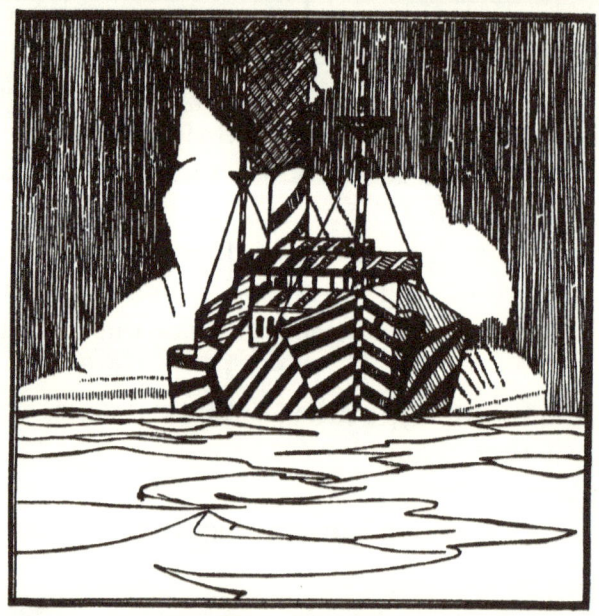

FIGURE 58. Thrusts and Their Effect on Volume

and robbing the form of its vertical significance. Clearly enough, there is no harmonious relation between the thrusts and the enclosing structural lines; the honesty, directness, of the structure is neutralized—destroyed!

How effective thrusts unrelated to the structure may become as causes leading to warped and distorted structure, is shown in Figure 58, in which a camouflaged ship has its volume completely obliterated, naturally by intent.

In *B*, Figure 57, the outer rectangle or enclosure has its upward thrust *supported* by the interior divisions. In this example, the enclosure and corresponding spaces and lines work together in the same direction, making the rectangle appear in its true, unwarped form, but higher than *A*, although of the same height. Here is an example of two thrusts working together for a common end, with very little in the way of horizontal lines as counter or balancing thrusts, a pattern in which apparent added height and lightness are augmented, giving more significance to the area.

Thus a clever designer may completely balance his thrusts; may make one thrust dominate slightly; or he may let one powerful thrust so predominate that it seems actually to push the form—to distend it in the direction of the major thrust. Interior decorators and dress designers use this effective device of playing thrust and counter thrust against each other, reducing and increasing apparent heights at will, but maintaining a balance and structural integrity.

In *C*, the thrust, 2, and counter thrust, *1*, keep the structure intact and in equal-thrust balance; while in *D* there is an equal or static, formal balance of all forces which spells monotony, unless counteracted by other forces. In *E* and *F*, Figure 57, are examples of thrusts and counter thrusts similar to *B* and *C*, but applied to horizontal planes: *E* shows an augmented thrust; *F*, a thrust neutralized.

Summarizing balance principles to this point, we can say that the strength of harmonious unity in the appearance of a piece of furniture depends upon the force and number of balanced movements or thrusts in contrasting or parallel movements and the proportions and number of balanced masses and spaces. Apparently thrusts have much to do with the significant meaning in line described in the previous chapter.

In modern design, each table top, shelf, inlay, support, shadow—in fact, all masses and spaces—exert thrusts which must be approximately balanced; yet we cannot destroy the significance of the volume. The following suggestions will aid in producing this type of balance:

1. Some major spaces and masses must, by their direction, support the major thrust of the volume.

2. Counter thrusts, while aiding to balance the major thrust, must not neutralize it.

Study the thrust balance of Figures 22, 23, and 58a, and, in these architectural examples, try to sense the thrust plan. A decided lack of balance and loss of structure is shown in Figure 58, a camouflaged ship. In Figure 55, Plate 6, the thrust is horizontal and dominant, balanced but not neutralized by the verticals; while in Figure 51, the same horizontal movement persists, relieved by the vertical upright supports. In Figure 50, Plate 6, the table top and dark base strips give a horizontal thrust, balanced by the vertical front panels. Note the support given to the major thrusts by the wall bookcases in Figures 50 and 51.

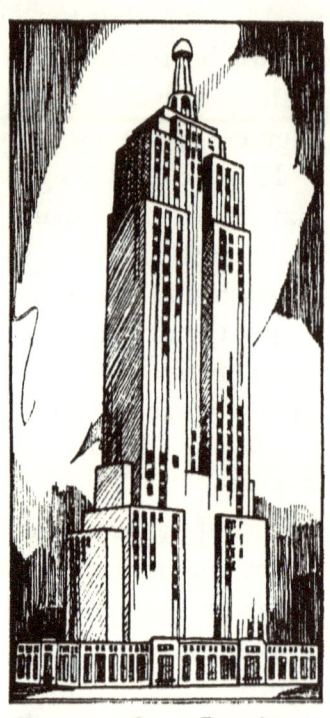

FIGURE 58a. Dominant Vertical Thrust Balanced by Horizontal Thrust

BALANCE OF TONE

The modern furniture designer, depending as he does upon shades and shadows produced by spaces and masses, needs both lighter and darker tones to complete his balance and to distribute tones in such a manner as to augment the thrust pattern. Thus, in Figure 50, Plate 6, dark bands balance masses of shadow and distribute darks throughout the design to accentuate the horizontal thrusts and to advance variety in the pattern. As in the child's cabinet of Plate 5, we found it expedient and more pleasing to add a band of dark tone to the base of the pattern; so, in a number of instances, a dark band or shadow at the base gives a sense of solidity and a balancing note to shelving shadows.

Here again, it is a matter of feeling as to just how lights and darks should be arranged. Each side of the project must be considered separately, yet integrated with the whole. The final result is checked by observing that weights (lights and darks) have been well distributed in balance and that the pattern, including shadows, does not seem to be too heavy at any one point or area; furthermore, that your tones support the spirit, the significance of the design, and carry out the line-and-mass plan of the whole, at the same time adding interest *through contrasts*. Current styles tend towards dark tones, either at the top, or more commonly at the base, of the volume; possibly at both points.

Color balance, normally considered with tonal balance, will be left for consideration with the final or form stage of design development.

CHAPTER SIX
PLASTIC FORMS
AND MATERIALS

THE term "plastic" means capable of being formed, molded, or modelled. Unquestionably then, wood, metal, and the new plastics, to be detailed later, possess qualities in varying degrees according to their physical structures.

In his book on *Modern Architecture,* Frank Lloyd Wright says, "Plasticity is of utmost importance. The word implies absence of constructed effects as evident in the result. This important word 'plastic' means that the quality and nature of materials are seen 'flowing or growing' into form instead of seen as built up out of cut-and-joined pieces. 'Composed' is the academic term for this academic process in furniture. 'Plastic' forms, however, are not 'composed' nor set up. They, happily, inasmuch as they are produced by a 'growing' process, must be developed . . . created."

In this text, starting with the volumetric casing, the designs grow into form by a truly creative process; and thus their development has been plastic, and the different parts of the pattern are integrated one with the other, and thus molded into a homogeneous plasticity. But in this text, the term "plasticity," while including the growth of the design out of the materials, will include the following quality: the actual appearance of furniture after being formed, molded or modelled, and the actual plastic possibilities of the different materials, as the flowing, growing qualities of metal, wood, and so on.

As we look at a piece of furniture, we realize its degree or stage of plasticity by means of its light and shadow, for without these, there would be no form for us to see. Important, too, for its plastic qualities, is color; for certain colors, as yellow and red, seem to advance, while blue and blue green are receding. Applied to furniture, they tend to mold or model it by causing certain parts to advance while others seem to recede. Experiments with colors applied to walls prove conclusively their capacity to enlarge or to contract room space; and, as space is important to the designer, color will be found to play an increasingly important rôle.

Paralleling the advance in the use of color, the element of plasticity daily is gaining attention. The vogue for box-like furniture with its nonplastic, stripped appearance is abandoned for greater plasticity.

To make this question of plasticity clear, for a moment let us think of the plastic qualities seen in types of period furniture. Queen Anne furniture, for example, represents a fully rounded plasticity, with many corners rounded off and genial rounded curves much in evidence, but with enrichment not flowing from the structure but something stuck on; while, in certain types of Louis Sixteenth furniture, plasticity developed far in excess of the material, with the inevitable consequences in weakened construction. By many, these fully rounded plastic patterns are considered as effeminate and little adapted to this, the machine age.

Much period furniture possessed light-and-shade qualities based on the cylinder and sphere, with fully rounded, bulbous forms and turned elements of great complexity. Indeed, wood was made to do many antics quite foreign to its plastic capacity.

Some contemporary designers look with disfavor upon the extreme plasticity of past periods, feeling it to be out of sympathy with the times, little fitting to the material, especially objecting to the misuse of materials, and naturally mistrusting plasticity which interferes with the proper functioning of an object. As a reaction from roundness and softness, modern designers lean toward simplicity, towards the crisp directness of straight lines, sharp angles, clean-cut, often deep shadows, and the glitter of brilliant high lights.

PLASTIC TYPES

At this design stage, it is necessary to study three types of plasticity prevalent in modern design. The first type of plasticity is termed the *blocked out*, and is characterized by a design in which the volume has been but slightly penetrated. disturbing its form by removing a small amount of space and leaving much more mass than space.

The plastic effect of this type of design, illustrated in Figure 53, Plate 6, and in Figures 66 and 75, pages 81 and 85, is that of permanence and dignity plus solidity. Its degree of plasticity is not particularly marked, and consists of sharp angles with their clear-cut shadows. To relieve the monotony of the large, unbroken surfaces, typical of this type, inlays and veneers are frequently utilized.

Analyzing the symmetrical clock case of Figure 53, Plate 6, shown only in its mass-and-space stage, we see a vertical thrust pattern, emphasized by recessed base, typical of the blocked-out type of plasticity, with the light and shade at the top balanced by the dark base band. The problem of space-and-mass balance enters into this blocked-out pattern as a minor problem.

The second type of plastic treatment is called *penetration*, in which the volumetric mass is penetrated frequently to considerable depth but rarely cut completely through the volume. In this type of plasticity, illustrated by Figures 50 and 54, Plate 6, much more space is removed, producing deeper shadows than is the case with blocked-out plasticity, and bringing with it problems of tonal balance directly concerned with these shadows. Penetration of the volume by space may be deep as in Figures 51 and 54, or moderate as in Figure 56; but, with either moderate or deep penetration, the amount of space removed from the volume is greater than in blocked-out plasticity, and the effect is towards lightness.

The third type of plasticity is *piercing,* in which space has cut completely through the volume. As space and light are becoming more and more emphasized, particularly in domestic architecture, this type of open furniture increasingly will be in demand. Figure 55, the volumetric mass and space plan for a window stand, is typical of this type of plasticity, allowing as it does, ready access and free passage of light and sunshine. Then, too, the pattern brings to us a sense of freedom, of freshness, of openness and lightness; but which must not be associated with structural weakness, a defect not tolerated by modern designers.

A variation of the pierced pattern is found in Figure 51, in which large sections of the volume are pierced by space, including the desk top as well as the shelving. Piercing may be in either the outer portion of the volume, in its interior, or both.

Comparing the three types of plastic expression herein presented with sculpture, there are the following analogies: blocking out with low relief sculpture, penetration with high relief, and "in the round" with piercing; while architectural, historical progression is marked with gradual progressions from the blocked out to the pierced, the over-pierced, and then back to penetration.

Plasticity is directly related to tone quality: In its deeply penetrated aspects, there are produced deep, rich shadows, usually crisp and sharp. While plastic modeling of the classic forms gave us the softly rounded moldings of the scotia, ovolo, and the cymas; modernism gives angular contours, frequently triangular or square in section, which of course, give in turn a tonal pattern of lights and shades differing from the traditional.

Recently, the traditionalists and modernists have approached a compromise in that a softening of contours and

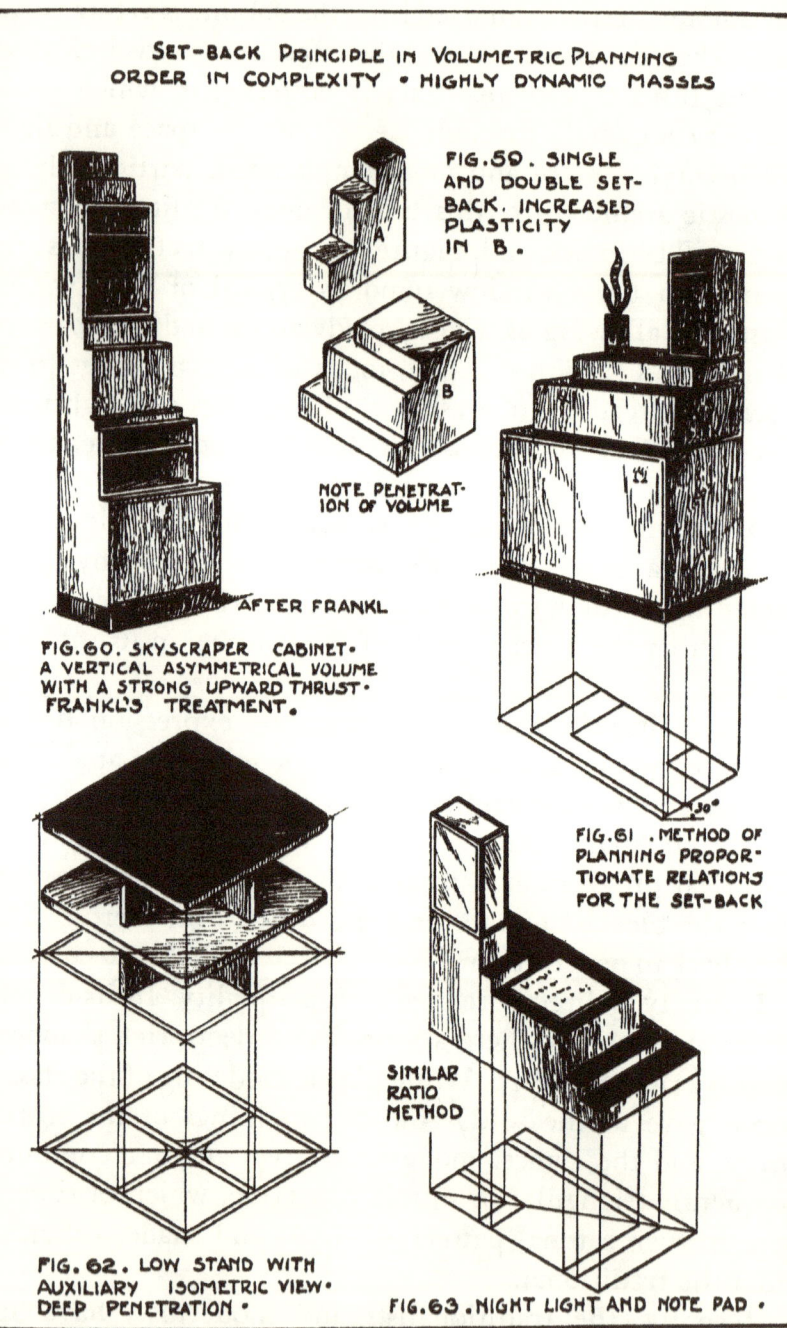

SET-BACK PRINCIPLE IN VOLUMETRIC PLANNING
ORDER IN COMPLEXITY • HIGHLY DYNAMIC MASSES

FIG.59. SINGLE AND DOUBLE SET-BACK. INCREASED PLASTICITY IN B.

A

B

NOTE PENETRATION OF VOLUME

AFTER FRANKL

FIG.60. SKYSCRAPER CABINET•
A VERTICAL ASYMMETRICAL VOLUME
WITH A STRONG UPWARD THRUST•
FRANKL'S TREATMENT.

FIG.61 .METHOD OF PLANNING PROPOR-TIONATE RELATIONS FOR THE SET-BACK

SIMILAR RATIO METHOD

FIG.62. LOW STAND WITH AUXILIARY ISOMETRIC VIEW•
DEEP PENETRATION •

FIG.63 .NIGHT LIGHT AND NOTE PAD •

Plate 7

planes makes permissible more rounded forms, which, with
their grace and beauty, are leading extreme light-and-shade
patterns away from extreme harshness into modulations,
and stimulating the "growing" qualities of plasticity.

But, whether the plastic effects are of the moderately
rounded or angular types, their shadows make tonal notes,
varying with the depth of penetration, and must be so
balanced as to produce a pleasing distribution.

In Figure 59, Plate 7, is an illustration of the increase in
varied plasticity by the introduction of double penetration
of the volume, that is, penetration from two directions. While
the painter has to represent plasticity on the single plane
of his canvas, the wood craftsman, like the sculptor, deals in
three-dimensional material; and in such examples as in
Figure 59, has excellent opportunities for creative expression
in a plastic medium, as long as he stays within the plastic
limitations of the material.

In Figure 60, Plate 7, a skyscraper cabinet illustrates the
plastic attractiveness of double penetration. Paul Frankl
has done much towards developing the set-back pattern, and
Figure 60 is a close approximation of his work. The design
has a strong, vertical volumetric thrust and, seen from the
front, is asymmetrical, with the sequential or rhythmic
progression plan of growth for masses and spaces. Popularly
known by its title of skyscraper, the design is an outcome of
New York building laws, as illustrated in the architectural
design of that city by which light, sunlight, and naturally
space for their passage to the lower stories of the building,
necessitated the set-back of top masses. Though dominantly
vertical, Figure 60 has horizontal divisions, giving the sense
of compression, while the vertical masses supply the release
from compression or mass flow. Thus thrust and counter
thrust make for balance of thrusts.

The skyscraper design is an example of penetration without much piercing, with typical tone and space balance.

AIDS FOR SYSTEMATIC PLANNING OF MASS-AND-SPACE DIVISIONS

Realizing the difficulty of space-and-mass planning, there has been developed in Figures 61, 62, and 63, by means of auxiliary views which will aid beginners in limiting spaces and masses, devices for studying, for estimating, and for visualizing proportionate relationships, at least as far as the isometric plan view is concerned.

In Figure 61, Plate 7, a plan of the base of the volume has been drawn in modified isometric as explained in this text. Within the rectangular base of Figure 61, other rectangles were planned in interesting proportionate relationship to the enclosing rectangle of the isometric plan. These rectangles limit the left and right ends and center edges of the masses shown above. By projecting points in these rectangles to their appropriate edges, either the perspective or the isometric view may be constructed. Heights are left to the designer, who estimates them in relation to the points projected from his plan and within the volume, not shown in Figure 61.

Similar auxiliary plans are shown in Figures 62 and 63. Figure 61 is in perspective, while Figures 62 and 63 are in modified isometric. In Figure 61, dark areas mark the tops of the steps and supply an interesting tonal balance to the design.

Analytically considered, the thrusts of Figure 61 are mainly horizontal, contrasted and brought into equilibrium by the vertical minor mass at the top. Simple vases or figures will bring this top member into harmony with the lower parts. In plastic analysis, the entire design belongs to the rather deeply blocked-out type, with the minor masses showing deep penetration. The solid and compact form of this design is characteristic of the blocked-out plastic mold.

Figure 62 is that type of plasticity generated by a deeply

penetrated volume, almost pierced in its outer areas by space. The lightness of pattern inherent in this type of plasticity—lightness with some solidity—is clearly evident. A touch of style, of individualism, is supplied by the black glass mirrored top, which must be tonally balanced by the shadows below the stand.

As a study the thrust pattern of Figure 62 is rather interesting. The top, a square, is purely static in its thrusts and proportions, but the small partitions give a lively counter thrust which seems to supply life and vitality to the static top member. The auxiliary isometric view and its connection with the isometric is self-evident. A stand of this type is planned deliberately as a static form to stabilize and form an attention-arresting point in the plan of a dynamic room.

In Figure 63 is a double-duty object—a low-candle-power night light with a paper pad for telephone calls, notes, and other necessary night communications. The auxiliary isometric view contains rectangles for the setback theme of the design, with the diagonal assuring the similarity of the proportionate relationships of the base rectangles as detailed in Plate 4, Figures 40 and 41. Belonging as it does to the deeply penetrated class, it is an example of double penetration and the modeling inherent in the type.

All patterns on Plate 7 are typical of modernism with simple, direct, and functioning parts, and all must be planned within a volumetric casing, an unvarying procedure. Clearly to illustrate plasticity, the examples on this plate have been carried into the form stage, to imply that modern space-and-mass planning is against that complexity which obscures construction and towards the simplicity which clarifies design and supports construction. Throughout, the flowing quality of plasticity is emphasized by absence of obvious constructive features. In these instances, this term is construed as meaning the absence of legs, brackets, projecting table tops, and similar constructive parts.

THE NEW PLASTICS

As a phase of the growing interest in the natural and applied sciences, there has been evolved new materials known as plastics—synthetic substances made by combining certain chemicals into plastic masses capable of being molded under heat and pressure and frequently developing high decorative possibilities for the designer, while others are purely functional and adapted to machine parts or as electrical insulation.

For the designer, the most important are the phenolic resins. Popularly known under their trade names of bakelite, durez, resinox, durite, etc., they are composed chiefly of phenol and formaldehyde. Noninflammable, acid proof, tough and durable, they are used for radio cases, clocks, telephone instruments, door and cabinet knobs; while a host of new applications are awaiting the designer, challenging him in new forms, new functions, and new processes ready for his creative efforts.

The *phenolic resin group* may be cast into tubes, rods, and sheets, easily cut and carved and even turned into desired forms. While molded phenolic resins are limited in color range, the cast forms are obtainable in almost any range of color, and very often are amenable to decoration.

The *urea resin group*, known commercially as plaskon, unyte, and beetleware, and made from urea and formaldehyde, is used for cups, dishes, radio cabinets, etc., and has an unlimited color range.

Laminated plastics are sheets of paper, fabric, rubber, or fiber soaked in liquid plastic material with heat and pressure applied. Here is material for table tops, paneled walls, with growing decorative possibilities.

Other groups include the vingl resins, used for synthetic glass, etc.; the caseins; the inflammable nitrocelluloses, as pyralin, fiberoid, celluloid, and the cellulose acetates, used for lamp shades and other thin articles.

Many new uses will be found for plastics. Meanwhile they are available for inlays in other materials; or, as is the case with Micarta, a laminated plastic, become receptive of inlays. Dyed aluminum inlays in black micarda are brilliantly attractive. Many plastics can be supplied either in high gloss or attractive satin finish. Formica, another plastic, comes in many light shades; while the black material is effective for trays, inlaid with a bright contrasting metal.

OTHER NEW MATERIALS

Glass, metals, and mirrored glass are adding their quotas to the list of new materials and suggesting new forms and new construction. Vitrolite, a heavy, black glass, is growing in popularity. With their reflective properties and ability to extend the illusion of space, mirrors of different colors are bound to increase experiments into space extension; while plastics as means of securing tonal balance open attractive possibilities in the direction of sophisticated contrasts, as black and aluminum, black bakelite and monel metal, vitralite, aluminum and ebony, purple mirrors and glass.

Plasticity must always be within the possibilities of the material and never overstress its legitimate field. It is only by adhering to this rule that the atrocities of the past are avoided. Sticking a putty-like substance on wood or tacking metal patterns to it surely are not methods of developing plasticity that would have any appeal to a contemporary designer. Each material speaks to the designer; learn its language.

CHAPTER SEVEN
THE FORM STAGE
AND ITS ENRICHMENT

WITH an understanding of such basic principles as proportioning, balance, and plasticity, with some knowledge of plastic materials, we are now ready to enter into the last stage of contemporary design, that of form and its enrichment.

While the volumetric stage was concerned with the functional and aesthetic motives of the whole; while the mass-and-space stage dealt with structural fundamental elements, their pattern thrusts, balances, and rhythms; this, the last stage, deals with *methods of construction* and the *enrichment of the form*. In many instances, beautiful construction *is* the enrichment; but, due to the flowing, growing, plastic qualities of modern design, the construction is not obtrusive, and must not appear to be put together, piece by piece. Long, continuous, flowing lines, therefore, are much in evidence; secret dovetail joints, and excellent craftsmanship. These constructive points and their subordination to the spaces and masses, to light and shade, are a swing away from traditional forms in which emphasis was placed on such details as arms, legs, and so on, with these members frequently becoming elements carrying almost unsupportable weights of enrichment, as seen in the elaborately carved legs of the Empire period of furniture design.

Modernists feel that more beauty is to be obtained by simple beauty of line and mass of the volumetric subdivisions, rather than enrichment of the structural parts, which, from their point of view, tends to weaken rather than strengthen construction. Hence, durability becomes more and more possible as enrichment emphasis is transferred from constructive features to the large planes of the structure, and to emphasizing major thrusts and counter thrusts rather than leg, arm, and back details.

Modern embellishment, then, is simple and free from all forms making for weak construction or interfering with effective functioning. Dust-catching ornament is out of the picture. Delicately carved and frail furniture, current in the 90's, imitating hand-made furniture, but developed by the machine—in fact, broken and discarded furniture—is witness against these frailties. There is and has been much fine period furniture, well made and in every way attractive; but we are referring to the cheap, poorly constructed imitations, the stuffy Victorian red-plush affairs and whatnots, which surely were far from being perfect home furniture.

As this is the age of the machine, *the machine, then, should become a tool for producing beauty;* and, indeed, our fine veneers are a direct result of modern methods, while the flowing lines and plastic relations are products of the circular saw and jointer. Modernism advocates mass production, the spreading of enduring beauty in furniture design at low cost to all who desire it.

STYLE

Paul Frankl calls style a symbol of man's creative genius. Change is the life of style. Moreover, "style is an external expression of the inner spirit of a given time." Thus into our form-and-mass structure must be designed a freshness, directness, and stability, a freedom from the prejudice of past traditions which are considered wholly out of touch with this, the machine age. The machine must be considered, not as a vehicle of production, but as a means of mass creative production; and thus machine construction actually becomes the expression of the inner spirit of our present life, making the designer the master of the machine, not its slave.

THE FORM STAGE : LARGE VOLUMES.
ENRICHMENT BY ACCENTING CONTOURS IN SYMPATHY
WITH GENERAL THRUST.

NOTE MASS
AND SPACE
BALANCE

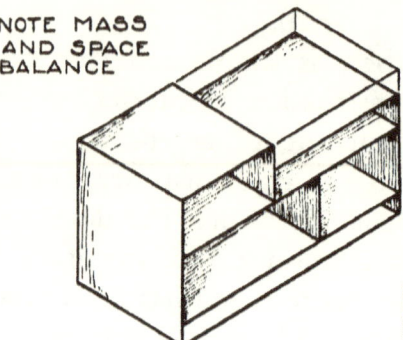

FIG. 65. FORM STAGE :
HORIZONTAL THRUST
DOMINANT: SIMPLE
ENRICHMENT BY ROUNDING
CONTOURS TO SUPPORT
THRUST.

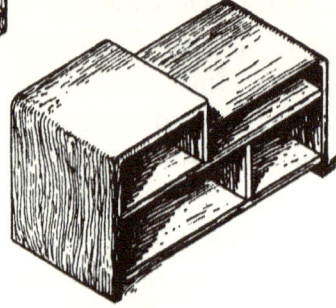

FIG. 64. BLOCKING OUT STAGE:
STRUCTURE PLANNED BY SPACES
AND MASSES WELL PROPORT-
IONED AND BALANCED.
DEEP PENETRATION.

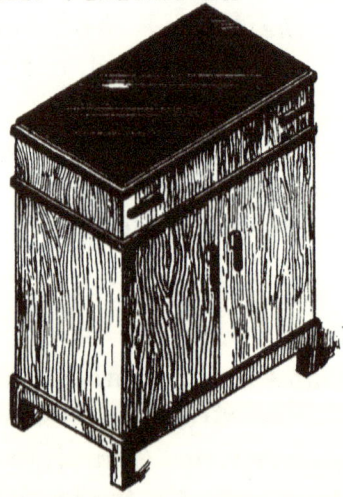

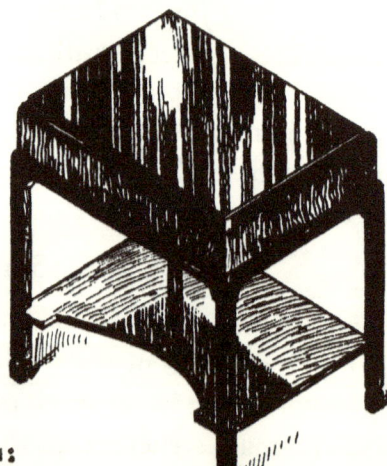

FIG. 66. SHALLOW PENETRATION:
APPENDAGES ACCENTUATING
THRUSTS. NOTE THRUST BALANCE
AND SHARP ANGLES.

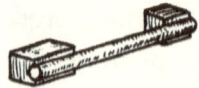

FIG. 68. HANDLE AS AN
ACCENTING APPENDAGE.

FIG. 67. ENRICHMENT BY
ACCENTED CONTOURS.
PATTERN SOFTER THAN
FIG. 66 BY USE OF CURVES.
LIGHTNESS THROUGH
PERFORATION.

Plate 8

While certain styles in this book may and probably will become obsolete (for style must change or die), the principles are sound and will lead to the creation of new forms in keeping with old and tried principles. This is an experimental age; and, in the spirit of this age, designers constantly are experimenting with new forms and materials out of which styles originate.

INTEGRATED ENRICHMENT

Throughout this chapter, the term "enrichment" rather than ornament has been used to designate the difference between the terms. The term "ornament" has been associated with decoration frequently more of less nonplastic, in that it was applied, rather than integrated, with the design. Enrichment, as used in this book, stands for increased beauty which does not interfere with function; and, what is very much to the point, it stands for beauty and enrichment which has been integrated with the design, is a part of it, or, to use a popular phrase, has been "built into" the furniture.

TECHNIQUE OF THE FORM STAGE

With the preceding paragraphs by way of preamble to the modern spirit of enrichment and of form, we can better understand the procedure. Referring to Figure 64, Plate 8, there is shown a low stand roughed out into its structural mass and space, with careful attention paid to the balancing of the pattern. In Figure 65, the form stands revealed, its constructive parts shown with sufficient clarity for design purposes.

It is not the purpose of this book to enter into details of construction, which may be obtained from many excellent books on the subject; nevertheless, it must again be repeated that constructive features, as separate parts, must neither be obviously concealed nor conspicuously prominent. The plasticity herein developed, that sense of growing and flowing of line, must be retained as a modern feature, a principle aided by letting the masses themselves become supports, as in Figures 99 and 100, with large silencers raising the mass from the floor. This, of course, does not do away with legs as supports; but, as we shall see, legs frequently extend in long lines, beyond their traditional terminations, to emphasize long, flowing lines of growth and the thrusts resulting from the typical modern construction.

MODES OF ENRICHMENT

There are three principal modes of enriching structure:

MODE 1. The first is developed by *placing emphasis on the attractive qualities of the materials of structure.* For example, the beauties of rare and native woods, used either in unbroken areas or in patterns, is typical of the mode. The uses of contrasting materials, glass and metal, metal and wood, wood and plastics, bring out sophisticated and brilliant effects very much in keeping with the steel and glass house of today, and equally attractive in more conservative residences.

MODE 2. The second form of enrichment is *by accentuating in various ways the general thrust of the volumetric mass* or by accentuating the thrusts of minor volumes. Bands of enamel, plastic bands, shadows, metal inlays, wood inlays: all are accenting media. Recently, appendages—small masses, as handles, knobs, and so on—have been radically changed in appearances; several handles may be combined to act as one mass and thus deliver a more powerful thrust than would several small handles, at the same time making for simplicity of pattern.

MODE 3. The third mode is by *relieving the monotony of plain surfaces.* Here we have a chance to use color, different materials, veneer, salient and sunken plastic forms, and many other simple devices which will be introduced as we advance in knowledge of new design processes.

SUBDIVISION OF MODES OF ENRICHMENT IN RELATION
TO THEIR EFFECTS ON MASSES

A. Surface Enrichment

The three modes of enrichment still further may be divided into two groups. The first is *surface enrichment,* which does not penetrate into the volume. Under this head comes the use of natural wood, veneering, and paint or enamel. The natural wood grain and veneers contribute to the surface textures (see Chapter Eight, page 91) and variety of movement frequently used to support major or minor thrusts. A rich variety of movement, ranging from the effects of line shown in straight, close-grained wood to the lively rhythms of the crotched patterns and burls, supplies vitality and life to support the dynamic volumes of modern conception.

Then, too, woods add the element of color and tone. Tone is defined in terms of the light and dark variations found in different degrees in wood graining and is not concerned with color, but with the light and dark aspects. Thus satinwood and ebony form startling tonal contrasts; mahogany and ebony, a quiet subdued effect; but, in the uses of veneers, it is well for the beginner to avoid extreme tonal contrasts and adopt moderate variations in tone. Small spots of dark or small areas of light will give sparkle in small objects; but one must remember that these elements of enrichment are classed as surface enrichment and are *not intended to give the effect of penetration or of projection of the volume.*

B. Plastic Enrichment

In the two groups of enrichment, the second deals with *plastic enrichment* or enrichment which is actually cut into the volume, giving the effect of light and shade, modelling and increasing the growing or flowing effect of the original character of the volume. As plastic enrichment is for beauty

FORM: TYPICAL CONSTRUCTIVE FEATURES
CONTRASTS BETWEEN OLD AND NEW FORMS.

FIG. 69. QUEEN ANNE   FIG. 70. MODERN   FIG. 71. MODERN ARM
LOW BOY: NOTE CURVED LEG. LEG CONSTRUCTION.   CONSTRUCTION.

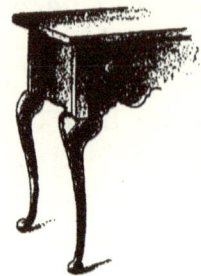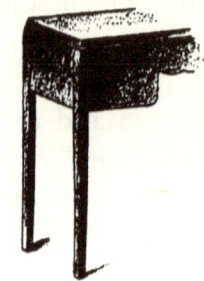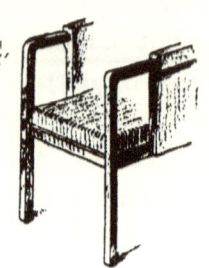

BROKEN LINES   LONG UNBROKEN   IMPRESSION OF
LOWBOY.   LINES.   ONE PIECE.

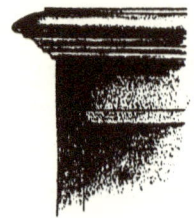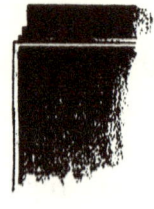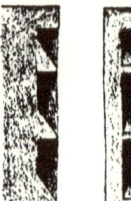

FIG. 72. CURVED   FIG. 73. MODERN   FIG. 74. MODERN
MOLDS.   MOLDING.   ENRICHMENT.

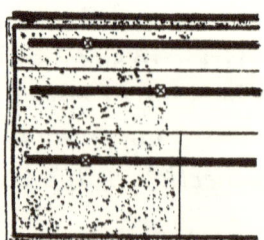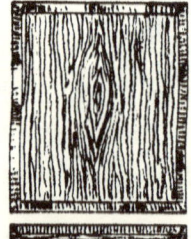

FIG. 75. EMPHASIS ON
FLAT PLANES AND LONG
CONTINUOUS LINES:
CAREFULLY DESIGNED
HARDWARE.

FIG.76 MATCHED VENEERS
FREQUENTLY OF
RARE WOODS.

Plate 9

and not structural in character, it must be kept subordinated and not too conspicuous.

In period furniture, this type of enrichment would be called carving, moldings, and so on; but, in modern design, plastic enrichment designed to become an integral part of the mass, is formed by allowing small areas of space to penetrate the volume, and does not have the "stuck on" appearance of certain enrichment of the more ornate French and other styles. Plate 13 gives the effect of the plastic ornament to which we are referring; while Plates 10 and 11 represent the first group or surface enrichment. Contrast the plates and get the feeling of the different types.

CONSTRUCTION

As construction is definitely and intimately bound to enrichment and to form, and frequently constitutes, together with structure, the major claim for beauty, we must set aside this section of the chapter for characteristics of construction:

1. A tendency for supporting members to emphasize their flow, thrust, or continuity. For example, arms and legs give the impression of one-piece construction throughout, with the inherent strength and dependability of this form of construction. This continuity is a marked characteristic of both wood and metal furniture; occasionally table legs are continued to the table top and through it. Figures 70 and 71, Plate 9 illustrate the simplicity of these patterns, contrasted with the broken lines and so-called sentimental curves of the Queen Anne lowboy, cabriolet leg, Figure 69, Plate 9. (Enrichment, Mode 2)

2. Emphasis is placed on long, unbroken lines, flat planes with little or no panelling, Figure 75, Plate 9, and Figure 66, Plate 8. (Enrichment, Mode 2)

3. Much attention is directed towards careful planning of functional details as knobs, handles, Figures 66 and 68, Plate 8. Details are planned either to parallel the major thrust

or to act as counterpoised parts of the design. (Enrichment, Mode 2)

4. Curved moldings and carving prevalent in period design of certain schools, as made visible by their lines, shadows, and cast shadows, are considered as too soft for the modern spirit. Figure 72 depicts the classic mold, while Figures 73 and 74 represent the crispness and sharpness of the modern. (Enrichment, Mode 3)

5. In response to the growing desire for more space and light, there seems to be a tendency towards piercing the volume to produce lightness. To produce illusions of more space, for their sparkle and brilliance, both clear and colored glass and clear and colored mirrors on walls and in furniture are entering the field. (Enrichment, Mode 1)

6. Use of veneers, Figure 76, Plate 9, is common practice to relieve the monotony of flat planes. This requires excellent cabinet work and finish which will develop the natural beauty of the wood. Staining cheap woods in imitation of more costly and rarer products is prohibited. Increasing attention to textures is noted. (Enrichment, Mode 3)

7. Use of striking color combinations and contrasts hitherto considered too daring for use, together with the avoidance of raw, crude colors. (Enrichment, Mode 3)

8. Growing use of upholstery in modern treatment, i.e., geometric and abstract designs with an avoidance of the realistic. Upholstery if possible, is removable for cleaning. (Enrichment, Mode 1)

9. A movement towards unit furniture is clearly indicated. (See Chapter Eleven, page 131.)

10. Metals and plastics are entering into both construction and decoration, indicating future construction of greater plasticity. (Enrichment, Mode 3)

11. The increasing use of glass in construction. Its glittering and clearly marked planes bring a vitality to the darker corners of the room, while its reflections pick up colors,

lights, and angles. Also structurally, it is fireproof, acid and waterproof, and is readily cleaned.

With three modes of enrichment in mind with their two subdivisions and, with the knowledge of structural characteristics, let us now study Figure 65, Plate 8, obviously a low container for magazines and small objects.

As a deeply penetrated plastic project, with interesting light and shade, there seems to be little or no need for extended enrichment. It seems better taste to restrict enrichment to Mode 1 by bringing out the qualities of wood through the finest of craftsmanship and finish. As the object is a horizontal volume, with its spaces and masses designed to support this theme, use Mode 2 to accentuate the prevailing thrust. Mode subdivision A, Surface Enrichment, predominates the pattern.

Sharp corners give undue severity, while the ninety-degree or right-angle corner holds the attention too long, tending to check the full enjoyment of the horizontals, which are prominent features of this design. By rounding off the front and rear edges, the horizontal movement of the thrust pattern is accentuated, and the softened result adds to the general beauty without becoming effeminate.

The remaining right angles are not objectionable and, by their duplication throughout the design, give harmony through unity plus a certain vigor in sharpness. Structural and constructive characteristics are plastic in that they support successfully the growth and flow of movement, without becoming too obviously constructive.

Figure 66, Plate 8, a slightly penetrated, almost "roughed-out" design, has little plasticity, at least as compared with Figure 65. Functionally, its services as a sealed container differ from Figure 65 and its pattern would therefore appear less plastic. The wood grain of Figure 66 gives the upward thrust to the pattern, Mode 2; while Mode 3, relieving the monotony of plain surfaces, calls for the introduction of sharp moldings, made by slightly sinking the main mass in blocked-out plasticity. Thrust balance is augmented by appendages and moldings, while the black top, enamelled or in bakelite, balances in tone the floor shadows.

In Figure 67, we have the effect of extensive piercing of the volumetric casing with its enhanced plastic qualities and lightness. This type of design, with its tendency towards curvature, harmonizes with period furniture possessing simple curvature in contours or outlines.

Figure 68 points out the trend in appendage design, and it may be said that, in details such as these, much ingenuity has been and will be shown in future designs. There are many ways of opening doors and drawers; knobs and handles of tradition are not necessarily the last and only answer; and the beginner can well try his skill at creative designing in this field, taking care, of course, to make the drawer or door pull completely functional.

CHAPTER EIGHT
TEXTURES AND VENEERS

THERE are two characteristics of modern construction and enrichment referred to in Chapter Seven which need further development: textures and veneers, including inlays. First, we need to know more of the little-understood subject of textures. While we may follow faithfully all characteristics heretofore considered, the product may be disliked—its beauty lacking perfection through failure to understand how to manipulate textural treatment.

TEXTURES

There are two inlets through which we receive impressions of beauty in the creative structure: (1) the sense of sight by which the image of the piece of furniture, its proportions, balance, plasticity, rhythm, tonal and color qualities are judged; and (2) the sense of touch, transmitting the "feel" or texture of the surfaces to the brain. Thus the optical and tactile senses operating together give the impression through which we evaluate the art qualities of the design.

Sight perception is recognized in its relation to seeing beauty, but we are just beginning to appreciate the impressions delivered by those sensitive media, the fingers. Everyone has noticed the tendency of people to touch surfaces, to run the fingers lightly over planes and edges. Museums are filled with "Do not touch" signs to curb this prevalent tendency.

The modern designer must create his designs in the language of his material. He believes that gilding, painting, heavily carving and twisting wood is *not its design language*. He believes in the *innate beauty of wood*—it has the *eye* appeal; if correctly handled, it appeals to the *touch;* while certain woods appeal to the sense of *smell.*

We are now beginning to know that a great deal of pleasure is derived from contact with pleasing surfaces and curves, and to appreciate them through the tactile sensation, through the touch. An experienced wood craftsman often gauges perfection of craftsmanship as final by rubbing his fingers along lines or over the surface of a board.

Due to their textural grains, woods have different feels; and, as there is a tendency to use bare surfaces minus filler or stains, similarly textured woods must be combined and correctly used. The finish of surfaces is equally important. Cheaply shellacked, sticky surfaces, or sticky wax, always destroys pleasing impressions, even in well-designed furniture. Glossy varnished and shiny, unvarnished finishes are disliked. Old furniture, with its finish secured by ages of use, gives one of the most attractive of tactile sensations.

Thus the modern designer avoids fillers in favor of finishes which retain, unchanged, the textures of the natural wood and the beauty of the material. Oiled and rubbed finishes are recommended, and even spraying with lacquer. On rare occasions, staining is permissible, provided it does not alter the texture or pattern of the wood grain.

For illustrative purposes, plane and finish some samples of nonporous or soft wood, such as pine, spruce, fir or cedar, and some porous or hard woods, like oak, walnut, mahogany, gum, maple, birch, or beech. Rub the fingers lightly over these surfaces and make a scale of the rough and smooth, arranging them from rough to smooth.

Compare the textural feel of the following veneers or solid woods: knotty pine and macawood, harewood and croton mahogany, flat-cut walnut and rosewood, oak and bird's-eye maple. Which harmonize in texture? Oil and rub the surfaces and check results with the naturally surfaced woods.

Cabinet woods should be left as near the natural finish as possible, avoiding finishes which tend to obliterate or to unduly exaggerate the grain. The object of the finish is to protect the wood from checking, shrinking, warping, insects, and decay—in other words, (1) to prevent moisture absorption, (2) to keep the color of any possible stain permanent, and (3) to bring out the best possible texture.

Thus, poor craftsmanship, as chisel and plane marks, rough sandpaper marks, lumps of glue, nail holes, and gummy, sticky varnish, are deadly menaces to fine texture.

TEXTURE HARMONY

Texture harmony is a key point of good enrichment; there must be a consistent textural feeling between the articles of furniture in the room and the setting.

Rough-textured walls and a brick fireplace call for the "feel" of *coarse-textured wood*, such as oak; while the fabrics should be similarly of rough texture with base-metal accessories, as iron, pewter and copper, and the color schemes harmonize with the textural pattern of the room.

Our comparative study of textures has contacted *smooth-textured woods,* such as mahogany, walnut, and others, with a *satiny touch response.* Furniture with this texture naturally goes with smooth walls, enamelled or painted trim, china, damasks, and silk; while light, clear tones, such as yellow or white, are desirable.

Other textures, neither satin smooth nor rough, may be used to soften the roughness of oak and the slickness of the clear-grained woods. Never combine in one piece of furniture woods of distinctly different texture. Depend upon your sense of touch, which is a reliable guide to harmony in textural surface enrichment.

Watch the experienced craftsman in wood; you will see his sensitive fingers rather than his eyes estimating both textural and form perfection.

Textures in Plastics and Metal

Many individuals like the feel of wood. It seems warm, mellow, and pleasant. The tactile reaction to a freshly planed, soft pine board is almost always pleasing, while to some the harder texture of new oak work is less satisfactory. Possibly this explains why old, hand-polished oak is much more mellow to the touch.

Strongly contrasting to this is the highly functional metal furniture. To some people, its feel is chilling and far from homelike; but, in offices, it no longer presents these objections. There is less antagonism to scratch-brushed surfaces than there is to the highly polished chromium plate, while the introduction of textiles for seats seems to make the textures more pleasing. Possibly the textural contrast between the metal and textiles gives a pleasing reaction.

Regarding plastics, people seem to like hard, polished surfaces as in bakelite, while other plastics which appear soapy in texture or slightly sticky are less liked.

Thus, it is readily seen how important the subtle but none-the-less imperative question of the tactile approach to beauty is becoming, particularly in modern design, with its increasingly large array of new materials.

As a final suggestion with regard to textures, we refer to that functionalism which must govern all questions of textural appropriateness. A piece of furniture intended for the kitchen has a different function from a design intended for the living room, while school furniture differs from that intended for the dining room. On occasion, paint must cover wood, metal must replace veneers; but no matter where the article functions, its texture in every part must be pleasing to the touch, appropriate to its use, and as durable as is inherent in the particular material used in its construction.

Veneering

The second characteristic of modern construction and enrichment referred to in Chapter Seven is the use of veneers.

As a form of enrichment, it falls under Mode 3, the embellishment of plain surfaces. The so-called "stripped architecture" is now appearing with enrichment; the soap-box design has departed; designers are turning to lighter, more attractive forms. Nothing has contributed so much to beauty in design than has the use of veneers, but their use in both construction and design needs justification.

Let us say that wherever it is possible, solid wood construction is the preferred method; but, under the following circumstances, veneering is justified.

Many people have a deeply rooted prejudice against veneering, regarding its use as a sham and a device for covering up inferior and cheap wood. Irresponsible salesmen have sold furniture, claiming it to be solid material, which later on turned out to be veneered, still further increasing the popular prejudice against its use.

These criticisms arise through attempts to misrepresent materials. Good veneered work must always show just what it is, and why it is used.

Moreover, heavy, brittle woods, due to their physical qualities, cannot be used except in the form of veneering. Furthermore, matched patterns of unusual beauty can be formed by veneers—patterns impossible to develop in solid material. As pottery is glazed to cover the raw surface of the biscuit and increase its beauty, so veneer may legitimately be used for the same purposes over cheaper, unattractively textured woods. Often veneered construction is really much better than the solid; less liable to warp and split.

VENEER PATTERNS

An endless variety of patterns may be developed by veneers, suitable for entire pieces of furniture or for details on table tops, drawer fronts, etc. In commercial practice, plain, less expensive veneer is placed on the side of furniture usually turned away from the spectator. As many pieces of modern furniture are to be seen and used from all sides, this practice cannot always be followed.

Without entering into detailed description of the preparation of veneers, two types may be mentioned: sawed and sliced veneers, with the latter usually preferred. The standard thickness of the sliced veneer is one eighth of an inch. Veneers more commonly used fall into three classes: crossbanding, plain unfigured, and face veneers. Face veneers are selected for their beauty of color, markings, and texture.

The grain markings show pleasing variations, from the straight and broken stripes to the swirl of the burl and crotch patterns. The price ranges are extensive; while different cuts of the same wood often vary surprisingly, depending upon factors described in the previous paragraph. As an illustration, maple has three figures: curly, blister, and bird's-eye, with varying prices. Beginners are urged to confine first attempts to the commoner, more pliable, and less brittle veneers; although modern designers seek the beauty inherent in rare woods.

Cores or backing may be formed of plywood or lumber which does not warp to a marked degree. Cross-banding is a sort of inexpensive base of veneer, placed between the core and the finish.

The main principle in pattern forming is the creation of a symmetrical or asymmetrical design composed of matched veneers, although there is a growing tendency away from matched stock. Typical methods of matching are found in the Figure 77 group, Plate 10. Figure 77A, side to side match-

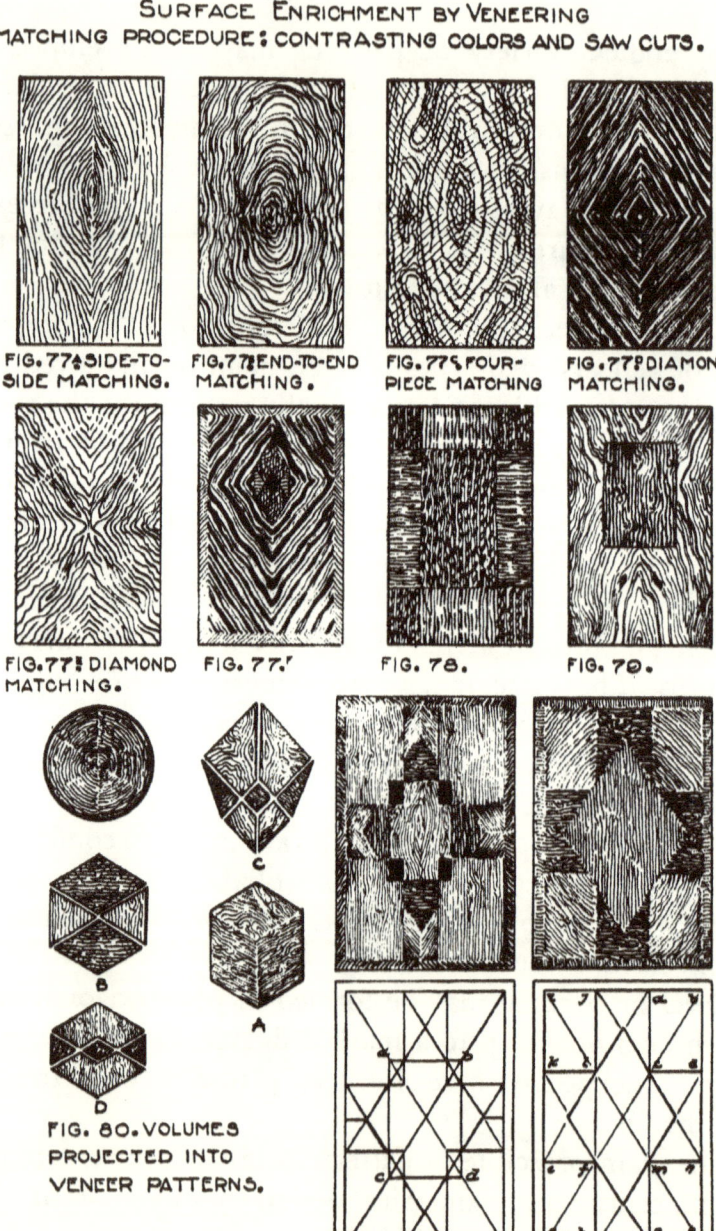

SURFACE ENRICHMENT BY VENEERING
MATCHING PROCEDURE: CONTRASTING COLORS AND SAW CUTS.

FIG. 77ª SIDE-TO-SIDE MATCHING.

FIG. 77ᵇ END-TO-END MATCHING.

FIG. 77ᶜ FOUR-PIECE MATCHING

FIG. 77ᵈ DIAMOND MATCHING.

FIG. 77ᵉ DIAMOND MATCHING.

FIG. 77.ᶠ

FIG. 78.

FIG. 79.

FIG. 80. VOLUMES PROJECTED INTO VENEER PATTERNS.

FIG. 81.

FIG. 82.

Plate 10

ing, is one of the simplest and most satisfactory; while Figures 77B to 77F are self-explanatory, matching methods. Occasionally, the diamond pattern is formed into the herringbone design, but its use is not to be encouraged.

Unit and Panel Veneer Design

Frequently a small veneered unit is advisable as an accent. This unit must be nonobjective; that is, of geometric or abstract character. Commercial inserts, such as sea shells, monograms, flowers, and fruit, should never be used, being out of spirit with the functional character of modern design. Panels are depicted in Figures 77F to 82, Plate 10.

Figure 80 suggests motives of the unit type. The circular insert is based on six segments of the hexagon, with the graining thrusts well planned to balance. The remaining inserts are based, rather appropriately, on the volumetric mass in its isometric rendering.

In Figure 80, A, is the isometric cube with its planes adapted to three pieces of veneer. In B, the same form has been used, with the top and invisible base used as two spots: the sides are obvious. In C, the base of the isometric cube A has been made smaller, while the forty-five degree triangle has been used. There is a slight hint of the original volumetric mass used as a basic form for the unit. D, Figure 80, is similar to A, but with a low rectangular form utilized.

The panels of Figures 81 and 82 are based on projective enrichment. In the panel of Figure 82, the diagonals are first drawn. In one corner, the rectangle a, b, c, d, is drawn, similar in proportion to the panel. A second rectangle is drawn at e, f, g, h, by connecting a, e; b, c, f, g; d, h; the original rectangle is projected or extended to the lower corner. The same procedure with i, j, k, l; m, n, o, p, gives us an underlying pattern or net upon which the veneered pattern directly above has been formed.

In Figure 81, the same procedure, varied by the rectangle

a, b, c, d, gives a pattern from which the veneered panel directly above has been evolved. The methods of Figures 80, 81, and 82 are suggested, not for the advanced designer, but for beginners, indicating, as they do, geometric types of desirable patterns. By varying the sizes of the rectangle, an almost unlimited number of differing designs are available; but the designer is urged to develop his own net.

Borders of veneer often are effective methods of surrounding panels, table tops, and similar objects, frequently appearing around the diamond pattern. Their grain planning is shown on the designs of Plate 10.

To avoid monotony, each section of a veneered design should show either *a contrast of grain direction or a difference of value or color.*

Rare and Common Woods

Quicker and cheaper transportation has brought to us from the world's markets a flood of new woods suitable for veneering. Some of the new varieties cannot be manufactured successfully into veneers, but a number have survived and are among the best species of cabinet woods. And so it is that we have these beautiful, new woods usable by reason of veneering when, as is now readily understood, solid woods would be both too expensive and inexpedient.

Popular Veneers

Modern Panels describes the more popular woods as follows:

Satinwood. This tree is a native of India and Ceylon and grows to moderate size. Most of the satinwood used in the United States comes from the East Indies. The wood is hard and of a light-yellow color with a rich, silky luster. The grain is close, straight, and sometimes mottled, and the wood is hard but works well.

Quartered Oak. About thirty-five of the fifty-three species of oak found in the United States are commercially useful. Of these, the white oak is most extensively used for furniture and veneering and has always been one of the most popular of native cabinet woods. It is hard, tough, and durable, with a handsome grain. The natural color of oak is light tan or yellow.

Orientalwood. The tree from which this fine wood comes is a native of Queensland, Australia, where it is used freely for cabinet work. It is known under several names; among them oriental walnut and Australian walnut. The wood is subject to wide variations in color and figure, varying from a pinkish background, with shades of brown stripes, to a deep brown with gray, pink, and brown stripes. The figures may be faint or strongly marked, and are usually broken, striped or mottled. The structure is open-pored, close-grained, and the wood works well.

Zebrawood. A product of the trees of West Africa, Zebrawood is fairly hard and dense but works well. The name is derived from the appearance of the wood when cut on the quarter, as the figure results in a series of parallel stripes—dark brown or black on a light-brown or tan background. It is often used as a border for setting off other woods.

Mahogany. The commercial name "mahogany" has been applied to several species of trees, about forty varieties being sold as mahogany. The African species is popular for veneers. The heartwood is a deep pink color when cut but turns to a rich, brownish red upon exposure to light. It usually shows a broken-stripe figure, alternating between light and dark shades.

Lacewood. This wood comes from Australia and is sometimes known as Australian silky oak. Usually rose brown in color, it has a slight luster and is marked by small flakes of light orange which stand out from the rest of the wood, giving almost a polka-dot design. Lacewood is moderately hard and heavy.

Japanese Tamo. Native of China and Japan, this wood is also known as Japanese or Manchurian ash. It is heavy and tough and in color ranges from light tan to a rich brown or light gray. Sometimes the figure is a narrow stripe and again it may be made up of all kinds of twists, curls, and whorls.

Curly Maple. There are a number of species of maple found in the United States, the sugar or hard maple furnishing practically all of the wood used for furniture and veneering. The wood is dense, heavy, strong, and very hard.

American Walnut. Another favorite wood for furniture, the American walnut is well known to architects and interior decorators. Of varying shades of dark and chocolate brown and marked by distinctive figures dependent upon the method of cutting, the wood can be used to obtain unusual and most effective designs. It is heavy, hard, and strong and works well.

LESSER KNOWN WOODS

English Harewood. Silvery gray in color, with a strong, rippled cross-mottled figure.

Prima Vera. A light yellow-colored wood. Some sections have a straight, striped figure; others a beautiful, broken, cross-mottled figure. It is used as a substitute for satinwood.

Brazilian Rosewood. In color, this wood is a rich brown; it has a straight grain. The wood is hard and produces an excellent texture.

East Indian Rosewood. A dark-purple wood with a straight stripe.

Macassar Ebony. A black wood with small white markings. Used effectively in modern design.

Macawood. Rich, reddish brown in color with darker, straight stripes fairly regular in placement.

COMMON WOODS

The commoner and less expensive woods are rich in beautiful figures and firm in texture. Usually sap knots, mineral streaks, and similar effects are excluded from matched veneers. In the list of common woods are found birch, pine, maple, cedar, oak, poplar, bass, chestnut, walnut, gum, and fir. Some of these woods are found in previous lists but this grouping gives the less expensive selection and affords ample opportunity for the beginner in design.

Certain common woods have a number of cuts available on the market; as quartered, rift-cut and flat-cut oak, curly and bird's-eye maple, figured flat-cut and figured quartered walnut, giving adequate variety in the low-cost range.

For the designer's convenience, different patterns are listed as follows:

Swirls: ash and oak.

Butts: (slightly distorted, parallel-grain pattern) ash, maple, and French walnut.

Crotches: avodaire, mahogany, oak, Brazilian rosewood, Circassian walnut.

Burls: ash, French elm, maple, poplar, redwood, Circassian walnut.

CHAPTER NINE
VENEERS, ENAMELS, AND
VOLUME ENRICHMENT

NONPENETRATING OR SURFACE ENRICHMENT

To still further clarify principles controlling the applications of veneers, refer to Plate 11. Let us again consider the functions of veneers in their task of relieving the plainness of bare areas, and by their grain design to give surfaces a lively, rhythmically dynamic quality or a restful, grain parallelism. This grain pattern as a whole must move in sympathy, in parallelism, with the major thrust, either of the surface upon which it is placed or with the thrust of the volume itself. Thus a horizontal volume should have most of the grain pattern in a horizontal direction; a vertical volume, a vertical grain, and so on. Circular swirls and burls are interesting on circular surfaces and, if cleverly used, make points of interest on any surface requiring a lively movement. Pieces of furniture designed specifically for rest need restful, even grains; while coffee tables, particularly with elliptical or circular tops, may well have swirling patterns.

As illustrated in Plate 11, Figures 85. 86, and 87 are exemplifications of these principles. Moreover, as the structural lines usually carry the major thrusts, veneering grain should support and augment the structure.

In Figure 83, Plate 11, we have a clock with simple volume enrichment of the blocked-out type. The clock face is a .618 or XM rectangle in a vertical position with the major thrust upward. The grain pattern is mainly upward, with the central strip making a slightly darker tonal contrast with the main tone of the veneer. Bounding this is a black veneer or inlay. Monotony of thrust is avoided and equilibrium secured by the contrasting top moldings.

In Figure 84, Plate 11, a side-to-side veneer has been used with a distinct curl to the grain. "Time moves on" seems to call for a lively grain. All touching parts of the veneer have opposing grain patterns, yet the upward thrust is dominant and amplified.

The book holder of Figure 88 has either an inlay or veneer of some dark wood to accent the outer contour; while a small panel, related proportionately to the end of the project, gives character to the design. Units planned as described in Figure 80 are adaptable to this panel.

Figures 83, 84, and 88, Plate 11, show darker veneer used in the contours to support thrusts and are effective border devices. In the three designs mentioned, it was felt that little plastic enrichment was necessary, due to the beauty of the veneering; but to keep them from appearing "boxy" or stripped, a small amount of blocked-out plastic enrichment is seen at the base and top of the clock of Figure 83, at the sides of Figure 84, and at the base of Figure 88. Even these conservative additions supply a certain modeling which adds to their beauty. Plastic and surface enrichment must not compete for supremacy in the same design; one must dominate.

TONAL BALANCE IN VENEERS AND ENAMELS

As has been repeatedly emphasized, darks and lights, dark and light veneers, should be distributed over the volumetric mass in pleasing arrangement, avoiding a one-sided appearance, the result of poor distribution and unbalance. Consider the uses of the design—Is it adapted to strong contrasts or to quiet effects with a close value range? While not sufficiently universal to be considered a rule, small articles like book ends, small boxes and paper cutters, will bear stronger contrasts than will large cabinets. Large volumes need to be held together, need to retain the attention, and violent con-

TYPES OF FORM ENRICHMENT
BLOCKED-OUT ACCENTS SUPPORTING THRUSTS.
SURFACE ENRICHMENT. BY EMPHASIZING QUALITIES OF
← COUNTER THRUST   MATERIALS.

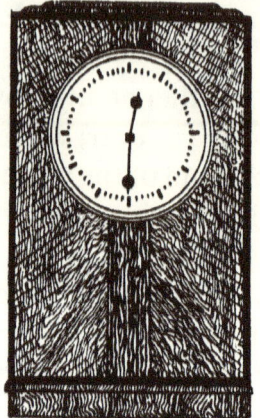

THRUST
IN 1.618+
VOLUMES.

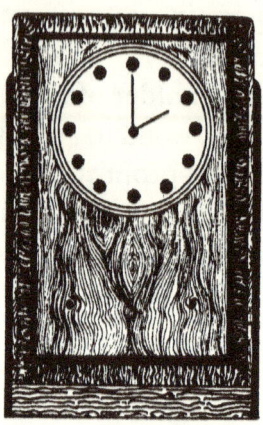

FIG. 83 . BLOCKED-OUT PLAS-
TICITY. INLAY AND VENEER .

FIG. 84 . BLOCKED-OUT PLAS-
TICITY. INLAY AND VENEER .

INLAYS AND VENEERS PREFERABLY SHOULD FOLLOW
LINES OF CONSTRUCTION AND EMPHASIZE THRUSTS .

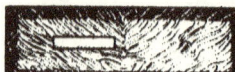

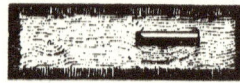

FIG. 85. VENEERS
NOT SUPPORTING
THRUST. C.F. FIG. 87.

FIG. 86. POOR
USE OF
INLAY.

FIG. 87. VENEERS SUP-
PORTING THRUST WITH
MINOR COUNTERTHRUST.

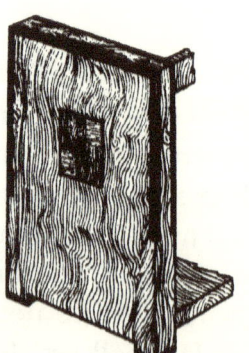

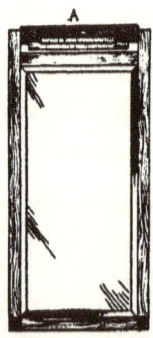

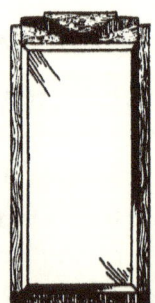

A

FIG. 88. BOOK HOLDER .
PANEL INLAYS FOR THRUST
ACCENTS POSTULATE :

FIG. 89. MIRROR
WITH TROUGH
LAMP.

FIG. 90. MIRROR FRAME
NOTE TONAL BALANCE.

AVOID HEAVY, CLUMSILY PROPORTIONED ACCENTS.

Plate 11

trasts in the values of veneers tend to destroy that unity so desirable in large forms. Then again, the skillful designer can introduce startling contrasts in large volumes and produce beauty as in Figure 96, Plate 12.

On the other hand, small objects readily comprehended at a glance may bear stronger and crisper contrasts of value without fear of breaking up the volume. The mirror frame of Figure 90, Plate 11, affords a splendid opportunity to balance values, with accents at top and corners. In Figure 89, a trough lamp at *A* illuminates the mirror and concentrates in one problem two distinct services.

Plate 12 continues with additional examples of veneering and various methods of surface enrichment. Figure 91 depends for its enrichment on veneering plus the upward thrust of the appendages or handles, small blocks of wood either enameled black or better still veneered, with their sides slightly recessed to give the fingers a necessary grip. The hangings in the rear of this figure illustrate the commonly used, horizontal motive.

The desk of Figure 92, Plate 12, has a close-grained wood pattern, with its vertical thrust supporting the vertical nature of the side members. The top is of plate glass with a gun-metal finish. Both Figures 91 and 92 mark a *growing tendency towards side matching,* which gives the effect of a series of parallel grains.

BANDS

Vigorous and crisp enameled bands and gun-metal mirrors, illustrated by the coffee table of Figure 94, Plate 12, are typically modern in spirit, while the curved lines give a degree of softness and help to emphasize the horizontal theme of the table. The "smartness," if one may use this term, is a trait or style which *has to be in the designer* and is a part of his creative endowment. In Figure 94, the finish of wood is to be texturally smooth and the wood hard, to harmonize

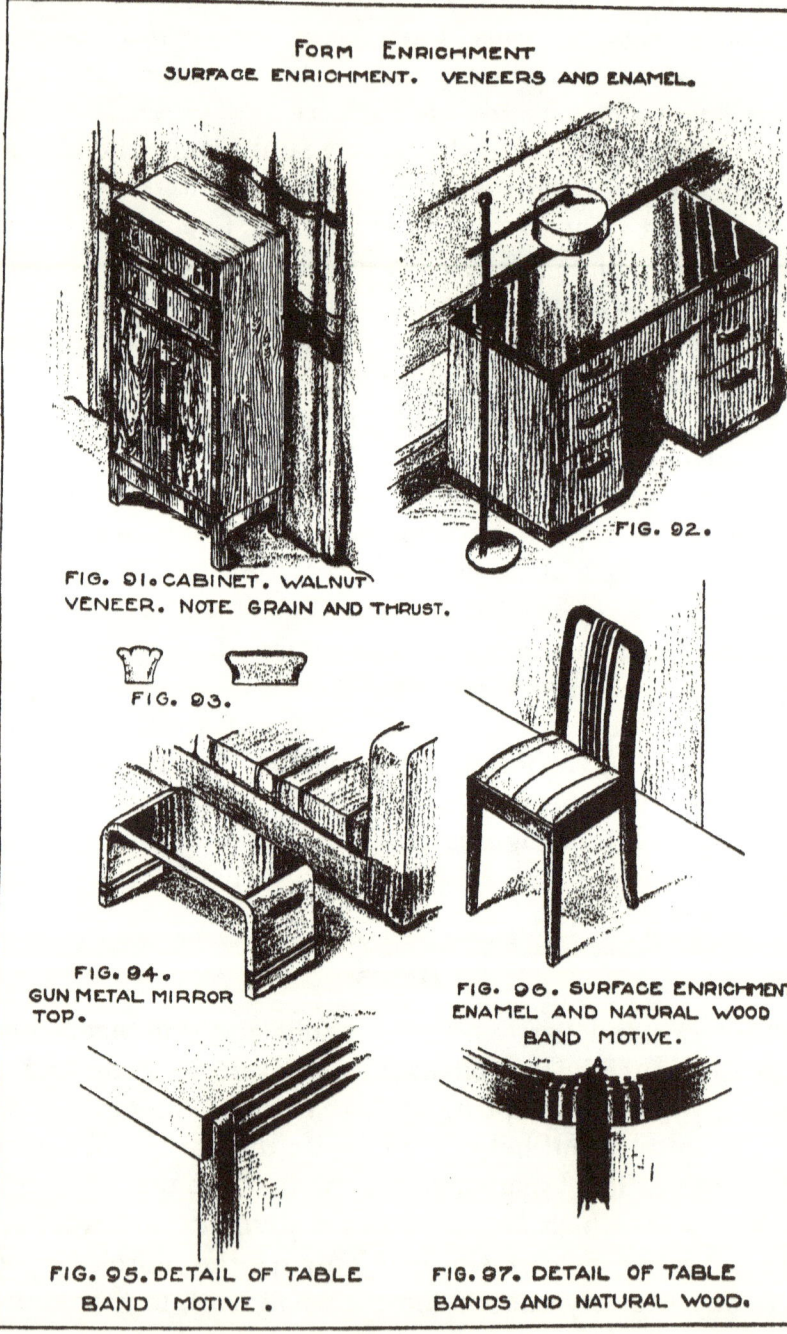

FORM ENRICHMENT
SURFACE ENRICHMENT. VENEERS AND ENAMEL.

FIG. 91. CABINET. WALNUT VENEER. NOTE GRAIN AND THRUST.

FIG. 92.

FIG. 93.

FIG. 94.
GUN METAL MIRROR TOP.

FIG. 96. SURFACE ENRICHMENT ENAMEL AND NATURAL WOOD BAND MOTIVE.

FIG. 95. DETAIL OF TABLE BAND MOTIVE.

FIG. 97. DETAIL OF TABLE BANDS AND NATURAL WOOD.

Plate 12

in textural feeling with the glass table top (oak and glass do not harmonize texturally), while the textures of the upholstery call for closely woven fabrics. Note the tonal balance of the top with the enamel bands.

The chair of Figure 96, Plate 12, with its veneered or enameled bands and tapestry seat, has a natural wood splat—a pattern appropriately repeated in the detail of the companion table of Figure 97.

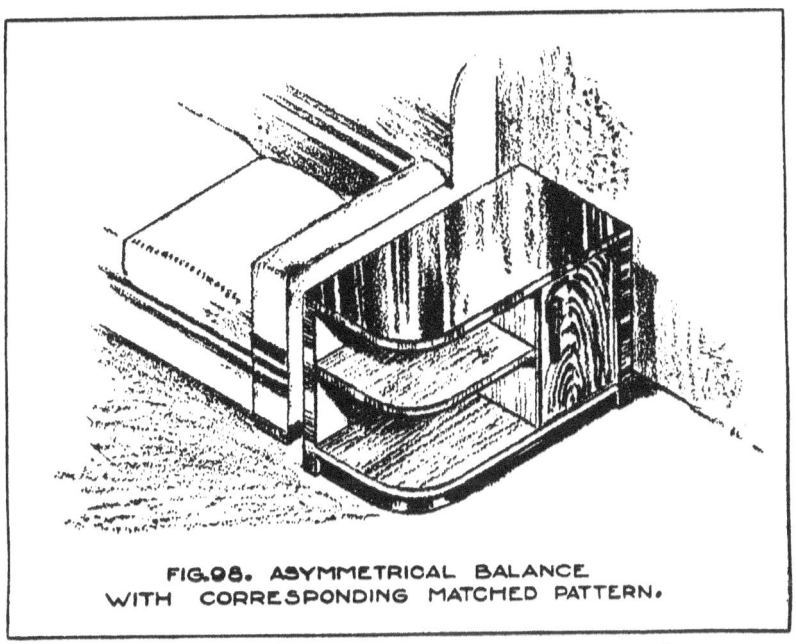

FIG. 98. ASYMMETRICAL BALANCE
WITH CORRESPONDING MATCHED PATTERN.

Bands, easily capable as they are of monotony in proportions, should be so spaced as to give varied proportions between bands. Whenever subjected to wear, use veneering or solid wood rather than enamel. Figure 95 gives an interesting bit of leg construction, while Figure 97 indicates a leg continuing through the table top as described in the section on construction.

ASYMMETRICAL TREATMENT OF VENEERS

Having presented a number of examples of matched veneers, one notices the fact that the surface matching of veneering usually is symmetrical; for example, side-to-side matching, with equal areas of veneer to the left and right of point of contact. Little experimental work has been done with *asymmetrical patterning*, and much beauty may be expected from this arrangement.

Let us study Figure 98, a pattern of distinctly asymmetrical character. Experimentally, side-to-side matching has been applied; but, with this difference —unequal areas are seen on each side of the door matching,

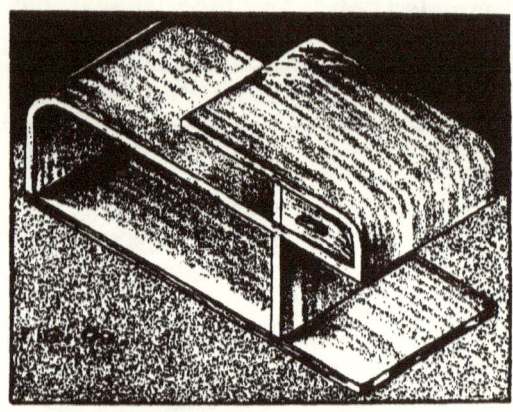

adding a touch of novelty, and adjusting the pattern of the veneer to that of the volume, thus establishing harmonious unity. Note, too, the counter thrusts in the vertical handles repeating the vertical uprights. Again, see the continuity of the textile bands in the couch, which pick up the lines of the end table, carrying on the thrusts and establishing unity between these closely associated articles.

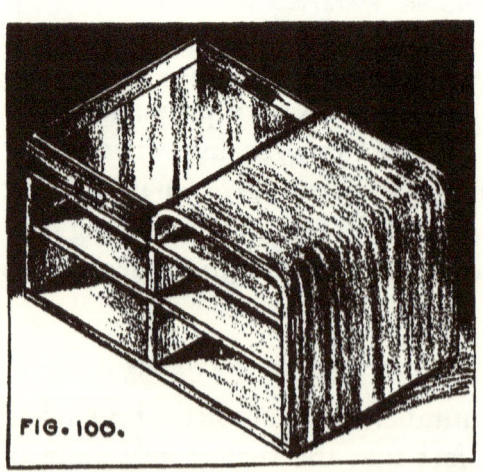

FIG. 100.

INVENTIVENESS

The popularity of low furniture, with its functional qualities, with its ability to give apparent added space to the room, has justified its design and opens up a vast field for creative effort. Figure 99 is typical of this pattern. The drawer can be pulled out from either side, thus making it available for its entire length, and eliminating the nuisance of locating something in the extreme end of a one-way drawer. A small snap catch centers the drawer in position.

If the designer feels that there is sufficient interest in his mass and space, solid wood is used, particularly if expense is to be considered. Figure 99 is an example of this type—a highly plastic design with penetration of light, giving the sense of space. A most interesting problem is the balancing of space and mass to supply this asymmetrical stand with stability and repose. Construction as an obvious part of the design is practically eliminated and long, horizontal pieces of wood carry the constructive thrust which must support the aesthetic thrust, illustrating plastic construction.

With the increasing interest in dual functioning of pieces of furniture, leading towards *a full utilization of all possible uses* connected with the problem, runs the increasingly growing emphasis upon invention: thus functioning can be regarded as not only including service but the satisfying results of beauty of design, which gives to the term "functioning" the broadest possible construction.

Thus in the low stand of Figure 100, it not only functions as a stand but its removable tray adds another service to the object, that of transportation, to its original job as a container. A loose glass plate in the bottom of the tray makes for quick cleaning. Asymmetrical in design, its design problems are quite similar to Figure 99—both should be equipped with silence buttons.

In both Figures 99 and 100, attention is directed to the short curves joining the vertical and the dominating horizontal thrusts. In place of the usual semicircles, these curves are elliptical, with the long axes of the ellipses running in sympathy with the major thrust. This treatment is superior in its dynamic qualities to the usual quarter circle; while

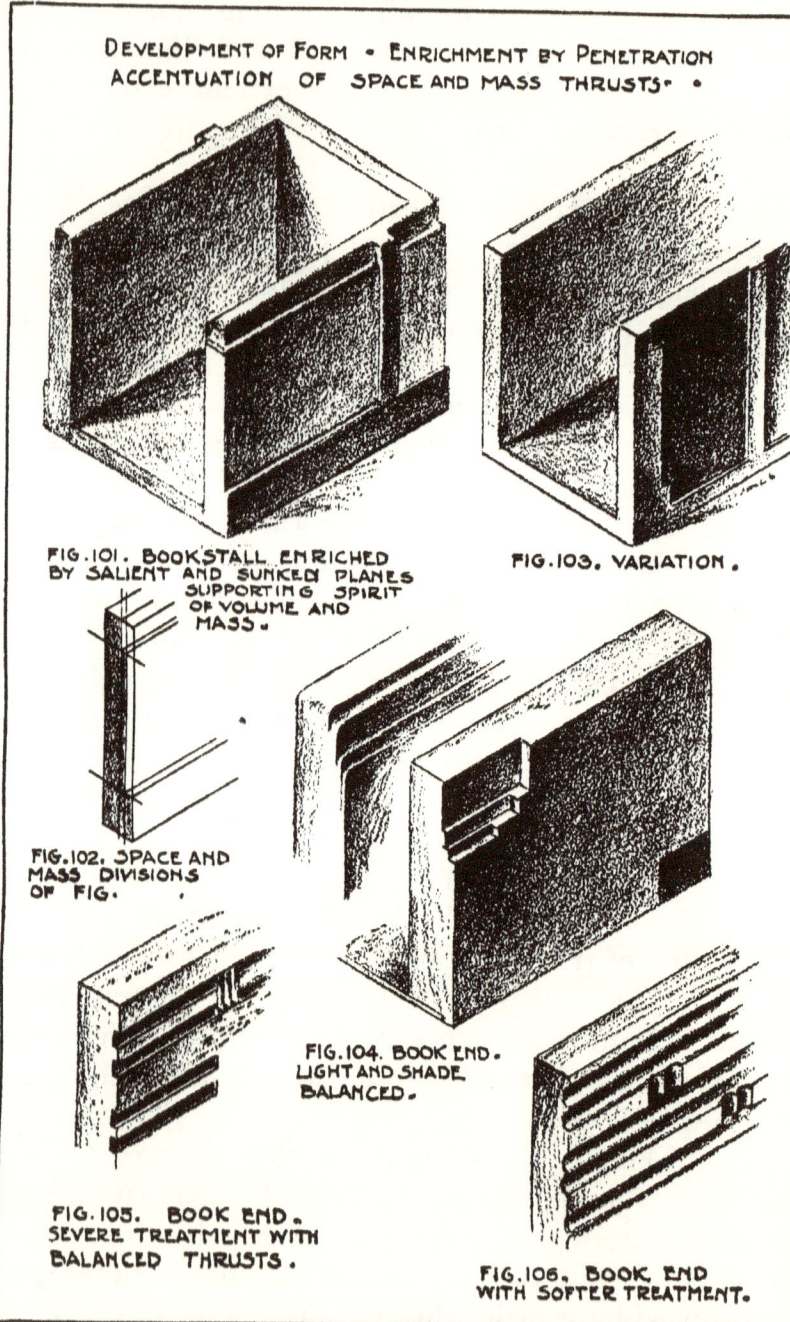

DEVELOPMENT OF FORM • ENRICHMENT BY PENETRATION
ACCENTUATION OF SPACE AND MASS THRUSTS• •

FIG.101. BOOKSTALL ENRICHED
BY SALIENT AND SUNKEN PLANES
SUPPORTING SPIRIT
OF VOLUME AND
MASS•

FIG.103. VARIATION.

FIG.102. SPACE AND
MASS DIVISIONS
OF FIG. •

FIG.104. BOOK END.
LIGHT AND SHADE
BALANCED.

FIG.105. BOOK END.
SEVERE TREATMENT WITH
BALANCED THRUSTS.

FIG.106. BOOK END
WITH SOFTER TREATMENT.

Plate 13

each quarter ellipse, constructively considered, is a separate piece of wood joined to the vertical and horizontal members. Note, too, the long pieces of wood in their relation to the containing volume.

PLASTIC ENRICHMENT

Up to this point, all enrichment mentioned in this chapter has been of the surface variety, with no penetration below the surface. We now enter into a phase of enrichment termed *"plastic,"* peculiarly effective when applied to *small surfaces* and small objects.

As described in Chapter Six, plasticity is the growing, flowing quality of a design, its effect of having evolved from the volume.

To clarify this idea, let us study the enrichment as shown on Plate 13. The article to be enriched is the bookstall for holding current books from which one is studying or reading. The horizontal and stable volume of the bookstall is deep, wide and high enough to serve its functional purpose, usually determined through measurements plus adjustment to make those proportions pleasing. An example of deep penetration, a box-like form with an open end, the bookstall is an object adapted to the simple and abstract enrichment of the modernist.

Figure 101, Plate 13, depicts one type of plastic pattern, formed mainly of one salient plane on a level of the original volume, and two sunken planes. The method of planning is shown in Figure 102, in which light lines across the end of the bookstall give the designer an opportunity to gauge his spatial relations. Deeply sunken planes would tend to destroy the feeling innate in this type of enrichment by subtracting too much space, creating dense shadows, and breaking up the volume until the oneness or unity of its form is lost. Then, too, deep enrichment will give the impression of loss of dependability and durability.

The sunken bands continuing around the object empha-size and are in sympathy with the horizontal thrust of the volume; but we must balance this horizontal band thrust by a vertical thrust which, while it does not completely neutral-ize the horizontal action, gives a satisfactory sense of sta-bility and thrust balance. This balance is supplied by the vertical band while its left and right placement is a matter of proportionate judgment.

The bands make the pattern more plastic or modeled and increase the interest and variety of the design. A slight round-ing of the corners makes for an attractive transition from the side planes to the top. This rounding does not by any means suggest an indiscriminate rounding of all edges, for a certain amount of square-cornered crispness is a characteristic of modern design.

A variation of the theme just shown is delineated in Figure 103, Plate 13, in which the vertical thrusts have been aug-mented; but the general thrust has been maintained by the base band. Figure 104 is a design for the ever-popular book end. The sunken-plane enrichment is planned in a manner similar to the method in Figure 102. For tonal balance, a small inlay is inserted to balance the light and shade gener-ated by the sunken panels. Notice the rhythmic progression in the use of planes—even in the small panel, thrusts and counter thrusts are planned with care. While Figure 104 is still classed as shallow penetration used as enrichment, it does not have the amount of space removed equal to that of Figure 101, and hence is less plastic, an effect readily ob-served by contrasting the two designs. Figures 105 and 106, Plate 13, are variations of the plastic theme, softened effects marking the characteristics of Figure 106.

The possibilities of shallow plastic enrichment are just beginning to be understood, and much creative work has to be accomplished. In no sense should this form of enrichment be confused with carving seen in period furniture. Plastic enrichment must be developed in the spirit of the material and with knowledge of the grain of the wood; it is geometric and abstract in character, depends upon its fine proportioning and interesting light and shade, and must not penetrate the wood far enough to destroy the volumetric unity. Moreover its salient and sunken planes must always be in relation to the major and minor thrusts, while soundly related to construction. Enrichment on modern buildings will give added incentives to the study of this attractive form of enrichment.

The abstractly handled human figure, revealed by salient and sunken planes, with thrusts and counter thrusts well balanced, is within the scope of plastic enrichment. The study of Egyptian low-relief decoration offers many suggestions for possible treatment.

CHAPTER TEN

NEW MATERIALS
AND NEW FORMS

METAL AND GLASS FURNITURE

WHEN we walk through rooms mellow with the tones of old furniture, rich in its historical traditions, possibly endeared to us through years of sentimental associations, it is hard to conceive of furniture other than wood.

But, overhead is the burr of an air liner. Moving across a rather dark room to its heavily draped window, we see a trimly dressed young couple emerging from a glittering steel and glass house, a house filled with sunlight and air and space, an efficient and inexpensive dwelling of modern design. Through the windows of this house gleam sparkling high lights of metal and glass. Somehow that house seems to stand as a symbol of the age—the machine age, the age of metals—and we wonder if a mechanical civilization will in the end spell the departure of wood for our furnishings.

For, in the use of metal, there are many advantages: it is superior to wood in strength, malleability; it is noninflammable and will neither warp, crack, nor, if rightly constructed, break at the joints.

Metal stands for what it is, honest and simple, giving lightness and strength and, with the recent addition of spring steel for furniture, a maximum of comfort. Thus we can argue that it is an efficient material for furniture. And yet, the argument that metal is cold and lacking in that which may be termed companionship, may be mainly a question of textures and tactile reactions. Many people object to pipe-like furniture as suggestive of plumbing and best adapted to offices and for the porch; but again this may be a matter of design and too vivid associations with dentists and plumbers. At any rate, its comparative newness places it in the experimental field, where its marked fitness and durability will give ample opportunity to prove its worth.

One of the most important decorative finishes is chromium plate, which has put metal furniture "on the map." Chemists have discovered some "cold dip" colors on solid or plated metals: copper and brass can be colored brown, green, blue-black, or "old English," giving agreeable and lasting variations of the natural colors; experiments are giving new effects to the designer, which may do much to remove prejudice against existing types. At any rate, metal is appropriate for the modern concrete and glass dwelling, both in textural feel and in harmonious relationship to the materials of construction.

On Plate 14 are found typical contemporaneous forms combining metal, glass, tapestries, bakelite, monel metal, and wood. From the designer's angle, metal furniture is capable of much more space penetration than is the case with wood, due naturally to the nature and strength of metal. If properly designed, a chair can be planned in metal to weigh about the same as one of wood, while aluminum tubing will give a lighter article. (Recent aluminum furniture exactly following wood lines is to be considered as imitation not in keeping with the qualities of metal.)

Another characteristic of metal furniture is in the growing use of curves, undoubtedly due to the greater pliability of metal over wood and the temptation to soften the severity of earlier wood forms. Will the use of curves change the spirit of modern design into an approach to the sentimental? The answer seems to be in the material itself. No one would ever accuse metal of generating sentimental attachments, unless it be in some pure art form, as sculpture.

In modern design, metal frequently serves as a graceful

FORM ENRICHMENT

ENRICHMENT GROWING OUT OF MATERIALS AND CONSTRUCTION.

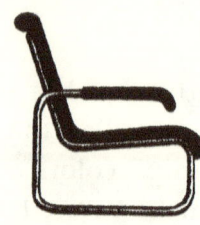

FIG. 107. AFTER DESIGN OF M. BREUER. TUBULAR STEEL AND LEATHER.

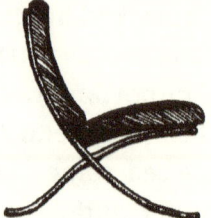

FIG. 108. CANTILEVER PRINCIPLE OF ROHE: STRAP STOCK.

GLASS AND SPACE

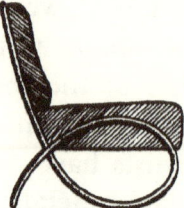

FIG. 109. LOEWY'S AND SIMONSON'S DESIGN IN GUN-METAL FINISH.

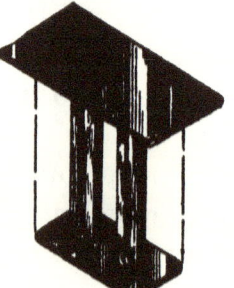

FIG. 110. BAKELITE AND HEXAGONAL MONEL METAL TUBING.

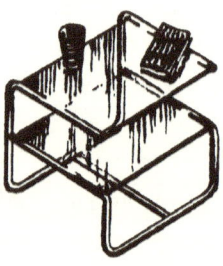

FIG. 111. CHROMIUM AND GLASS MAXIMUM SPACE DESIGNING. PROPORTIONING OF MAJOR IMPORTANCE.

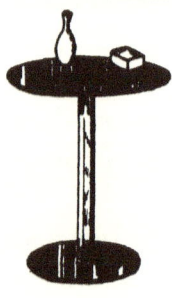

FIG. 112. BLACK NICKEL AND MONEL METAL.

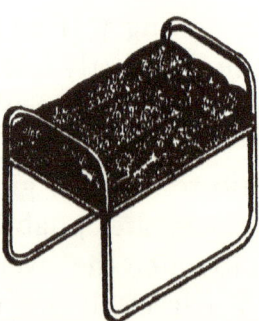

FIG. 113. STOOL: WITH SLIGHT CHANGE OF PATTERN, GLASS MAY BE SUBSTITUTED FOR THE CUSHION.

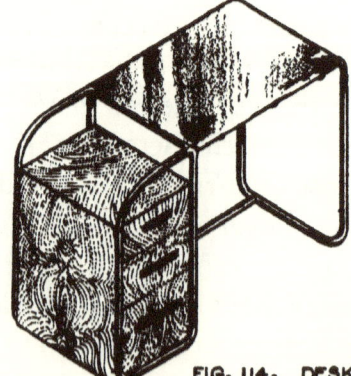

FIG. 114. DESK: CHROMIUM, VENEER, EBONY FITTINGS.

Plate 14

framework or support for removable cushions which may be readily taken out and cleaned or replaced.

In designing modern furniture, the volumetric casing is created and the mass and space divisions planned as with wood, each division line being regarded as the center line of tubing. The turning points of curves are proportionate indicators of subtle spacing, while the curves themselves should not be parts of circles. Ellipses, ovals, parabolas, hyperbolas: all make attractive curves which, in their beauty, far exceed the circle. The circle has one continuous thrust and is the emblem of continuity or concentration, while the ellipse has a varied and more beautiful thrust pattern.

And in designing metal furniture, the thrusts are much more complex than in the simpler wood forms; but, as is the case with wood design, there should be one major thrust responding to the character of the volume and, if possible, supported by one or more long pieces of tubing to give the necessary character to the design.

To show the versatility of designers, note the chairs, Figures 107, 108, and 109, Plate 14. Figure 107 gives the comfort of the rocker without the danger of its counterpart in wood; Figure 108, the creation of Mr. Rohde, balances on one point as in the cantilever form of construction; while the curves of Figure 109 are peculiarly attractive. The problem of physical balance in metal furniture construction introduces engineering problems, and supplies a splendid example of the link between science and art.

The sophisticated, contrasting effects of black bakelite and monel metal appears in Figures 110 and 112. As described by its manufacturers, monel metal, one of the new, rustless products on the market, is approximately two-thirds nickel and one-third copper. Monel metal is classed as a distinctly white metal more closely related to platinum in color and reflectivity than to any other well-known metal. It can be formed, machined, spun, drawn, brazed, soldered with silver solder, and welded.

Monel metal is obtained in various degrees of hardness and resists corrosion to a marked degree. It may be obtained in sheets ranging from .018″ to ¼″. Strips are available in thickness from .01″ to .15″. Seamless tubes are available with

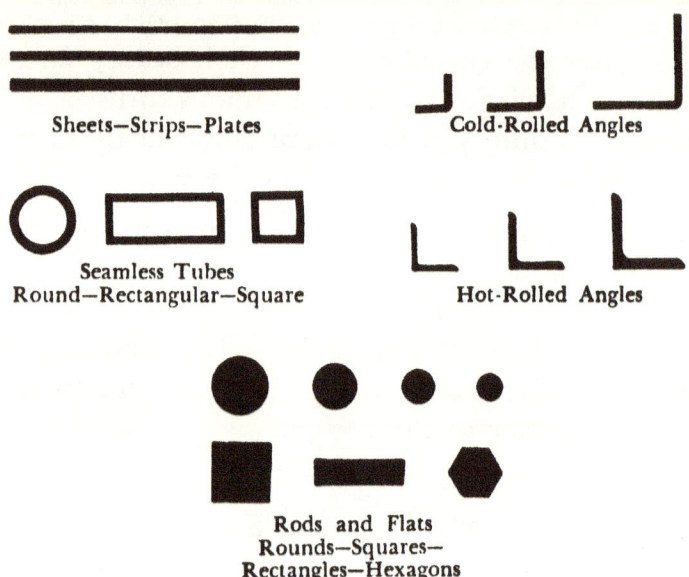

Sheets—Strips—Plates

Cold-Rolled Angles

Seamless Tubes
Round—Rectangular—Square

Hot-Rolled Angles

Rods and Flats
Rounds—Squares—
Rectangles—Hexagons

FIGURE 110a. Standard Forms of Monel Metal

outside diameter from ½″ to 2¼″, and in many shapes, Figure 110a. These tubes may be bent and coiled, particularly if annealed tubing is specified. This brief description of monel metal gives an indication of the possibilities in other materials on the market, as aluminum and other rustless metals.

Many finishes are available, as wire scratch brush, satin, and bright, giving various textures which must be considered in relation to the accessories surrounding the articles. For example, rough-textured wrought iron must be combined with a wood of rough, open texture, as oak. Metals capable of being forged, but with smooth textures, must be combined with close-fibered woods and veneers, thus establishing textural harmony. Large, thin sheets of metal, sandblasted into geometric patterns by the means of stencils, make unique modern screens. Here we find slightly differing textures in the same metal, defining the stenciled pattern.

A stool with many uses is depicted in Figure 113, Plate 14; while, by a slight change of proportions, a glass shelf, substituted for the cushion, converts the design into a useful and portable table. Convertible models providing dual uses for projects are well within the scope of modernism, distributing functionalism over a still wider range of activities. The dustless quality of the desk of Figure 114 has its distinct sphere of service for the school and office.

GLASS

The clear-cut alternating with the obscure in the appearance of a pane of glass gives it a peculiarly varied imaginative quality; while its textural relations to metal, its varied sparkle and light, its clean and hygienic properties offer to the designer material full of possibilities.

The reflective qualities of glass, its ability to pick up color, make it an attractive area upon which to place the colored glassware of modern service. Circular plates of glass without frames, utilized as mirrors, create illusions of new space and new vistas and do away with the stuffiness of small rooms; at least as far as reflections are able to add to room design their desirable quotas. Black and purple glass, vitrolite (a type of black glass), and the processes of sandblasting and etching, are enrichment features sure to bring fresh emphasis to the uses of this material for furniture design. Little is known relative to the use of glass for furniture in houses in which many children are living, and, on the whole, it seems advisable to omit its use under these conditions.

While other suggestions for the use of glass are found

throughout the text, Figure 111, Plate 14, is specifically an example of glass design. From the designer's angle, glass design gives a chance to use piercing with a certain amount of support supplied by glass; although the designer must not depend wholly upon this type of support, but avail himself of the firmer structure supplied by metal. This is illustrated by modern houses in which structural steel carries the load, while glass in the house corner gives a feeling of unity and at the same time gives light penetration.

Glossary for Glass

For convenience and general information, the following little known terminology for glass, compiled by the Plate Glass Manufacturers' Association, is appended. Mainly it deals with defects in glass and the amount permissible in different grades of the product.

Bubbles. Gas inclusions in any rolled glass. These inclusions are practically always spherical and brilliant in appearance. The term applies to all such inclusions larger than 1/32 inch in diameter. The term "small bubbles" (commonly known as boil) refers to sizes between 1/32 inch and 3/32 inch.

Seeds. Minute bubbles less than 1/32 inch in diameter. Fine seeds are visible only on close inspection, usually appearing as small, fine specks, and are an inherent defect in the best quality of plate glass.

Open Bubbles. Bubbles which have been broken into by grinding, leaving a hemispherical hole in the glass surface.

Skim. Streaks of dense seed with accompanying small bubbles.

Strings. Wavy, transparent lines appearing as though a thread of glass had been incorporated into the sheet.

Ream. An area of unhomogeneous glass incorporated into the sheet, producing a wavy appearance.

Scratches. Self-evident.

Short Finish. Insufficient polish or lack of brilliancy; improperly finished surface which has the appearance of being slightly pitted and wavy when the surface is viewed in reflected light.

Stones. An opaque or partly melted particle of rock, clay, or batch of ingredients imbedded in the glass.

Fire Cracks. Small cracks penetrating the surface, caused by sudden heating or chilling of the surface.

Sand Holes. Rough spots on the polished surface produced during coarse grinding that fine grinding did not later remove.

Central Area of Sheet. This term is used with slightly different interpretation with reference to plate or window glass. In plate glass the central area is considered to form an oval or circle centered on the sheet whose axes or diameters do not exceed 80 per cent of the overall dimensions. This allows for a fairly large amount of space at the corners, which may have imperfections not allowed in the central area.

Sizes and Thickness. Standards of thickness for plate glass shall be ⅛, 3/16, ¼, ⅜, ½, etc., inches. Polished plate glass of ⅛, ¼, and 3/16 inches thick is carried in stock in the larger cities. There is a tolerance of 1/32 inch per ⅛ inch in thickness allowed.

Qualities. All flat glass contains some imperfections, and the principle involved in grading is to exclude all defects that would be objectionable in a given grade. This is difficult, for there are no sharp lines of demarcation between grades, and experienced inspectors differ in judgment as to the quality of the glass as it approaches the limits of the grades. Small lights must be quite free from imperfections as compared with the larger. The center of any sheet, however, should be clear; whereas the edges may contain more pronounced defects.

Specifications are as follow:

FORM ENRICHMENT

CONTOUR ENRICHMENT IN METAL AND WOOD.

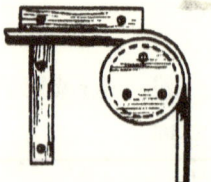

FIG. 115. JIG FOR
BENDING ALUMINUM
TUBING. SEE TEXT.

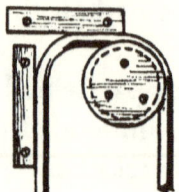

FIG. 116.
DOUBLE BEND.

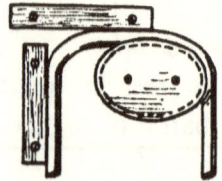

FIG. 117. SUBTLETY
OF CURVATURE IN
CONTOUR DESIGN.

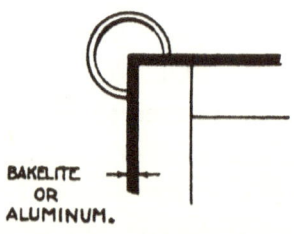

BAKELITE
OR
ALUMINUM.

FIG. 118.

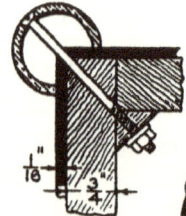

FIG. 119.

FIG. 120.

CONSTRUCTIVE FEATURES AND EFFECT ON PATTERN.
DURALUMINUM BOLTS AND SCREWS.

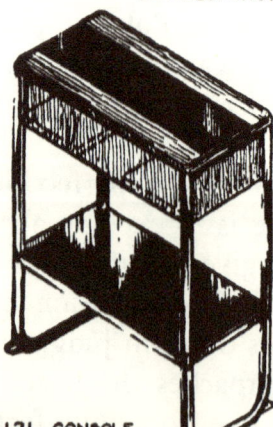

FIG. 121. CONSOLE
$\frac{7}{8}"$ AND $\frac{5}{8}"$ TUBULAR
ALUMINUM BAKELITE
AND PLYWOOD.

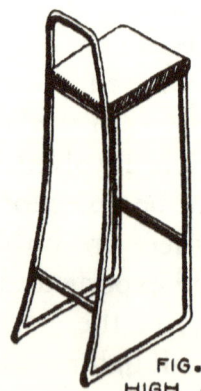

FIG. 122.
HIGH STOOLS
OF LEATHER AND NICKEL.
WELDED JOINTS.

Plate 15

AA Quality, A Quality, Number 1 Quality, Number 2 Quality, Number 3 Quality. Without entering into details of each quality, it may be said that the AA grade must be entirely free from major defects; only well-distributed, fine seed and small, fine hairlines when not grouped are permitted. Number 2 grade, for example, may contain the following defects: numerous scattered seed, occasional coarse seed, light reams, strings, light scratches, short finish if not torn, hairlines if not too densely grouped, and bulls' eyes if not visible from front inspection.

These classifications will give an approximate idea of the wide variation of permissible defects and will be of service to the purchaser. Window glass is considered too thin for furniture construction; but there is less expensive plate glass appearing on the market, although at present its maximum thickness is 9/64 of an inch.

METAL AND WOOD CONSTRUCTION

While this book is not planned to describe constructive processes, nevertheless occasional suggestions may prove valuable. Figures 115, 116, and 117, Plate 15, emphasize the bending of metal tubing. First the tube is filled with wet sand, the ends plugged, and the filled tube placed in the position indicated in any one of the three figures referred to, engaging the channeled jig forms. These pulley-like forms are quickly turned on the lathe out of hard wood and are valuable for simple bends. Figure 117 suggests an elliptical form, producing elliptical bends of greater beauty and dynamic force than the arcs of Figures 115 and 116.

Aluminum, stainless steel, or monel metal tubing similar to the material used in Figure 121 is cut for corners as shown in Figure 118, while the tubing is held in place as indicated in Figure 119. Wooden plugs driven into the tubing are used in holding secure the T joint of Figure 120. The growing use of masonite and plywoods for construction make for

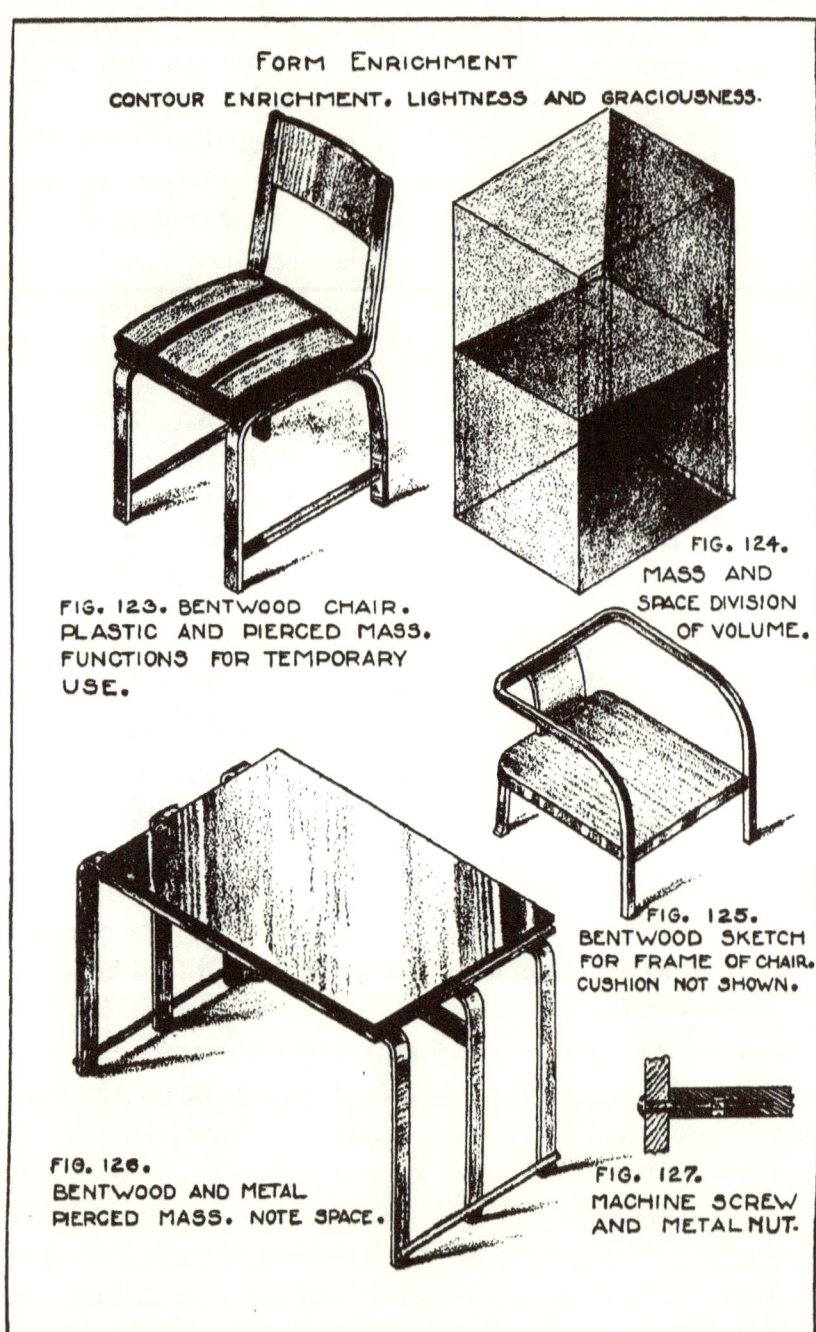

FORM ENRICHMENT

CONTOUR ENRICHMENT, LIGHTNESS AND GRACIOUSNESS.

FIG. 123. BENTWOOD CHAIR.
PLASTIC AND PIERCED MASS.
FUNCTIONS FOR TEMPORARY
USE.

FIG. 124.
MASS AND
SPACE DIVISION
OF VOLUME.

FIG. 125.
BENTWOOD SKETCH
FOR FRAME OF CHAIR.
CUSHION NOT SHOWN.

FIG. 126.
BENTWOOD AND METAL
PIERCED MASS. NOTE SPACE.

FIG. 127.
MACHINE SCREW
AND METAL NUT.

Plate 16

ready facing, either by thin sheets of metal, glass, bakelite, or similar materials.

The console of Figure 121 has two concealed shelves as indicated by the dotted lines, while the high chair of Figure 122 should be constructed with brazed joints. Long-curved tubing resting on the floor must have projections, as in Figures 121 and 122, particularly if any tendency towards rocking is noticed.

The enrichment features of the console and stool rest mainly in their construction plus accentuation and glitter inherent in the materials themselves. The movement towards the use of flat metal construction shown in Plate 16 seems significant of a move towards rectangular cross-sections in metal construction, which may have a marked bearing on furniture for home uses.

BENT WOOD

As styles move on, as new methods and new uses for old materials emerge, we see the advent of bent wood construction. By virtue of its process of formation, bent wood must have curves; its construction allows extensive piercing of the volume. Combine these factors and you have the air of graciousness and lightness so characteristic of bent wood furniture. With these characteristics, this type of furniture functions well in the recreation room, on the large porch, or the out-of-doors terrace and garden, and improvement in design may qualify it for the living room.

Figure 123, Plate 16, gives the design in its final or form stage; while Figure 124 shows the volumetric mass with its proportionate relationship problems, indicating the design process by which Figure 123 was planned. Another small constructive detail, a method of joining bent wood rails and legs, is depicted in Figure 127; while the steam chest is available for bending forms.

Figure 125, Plate 16, will suggest many ideas for chair con-

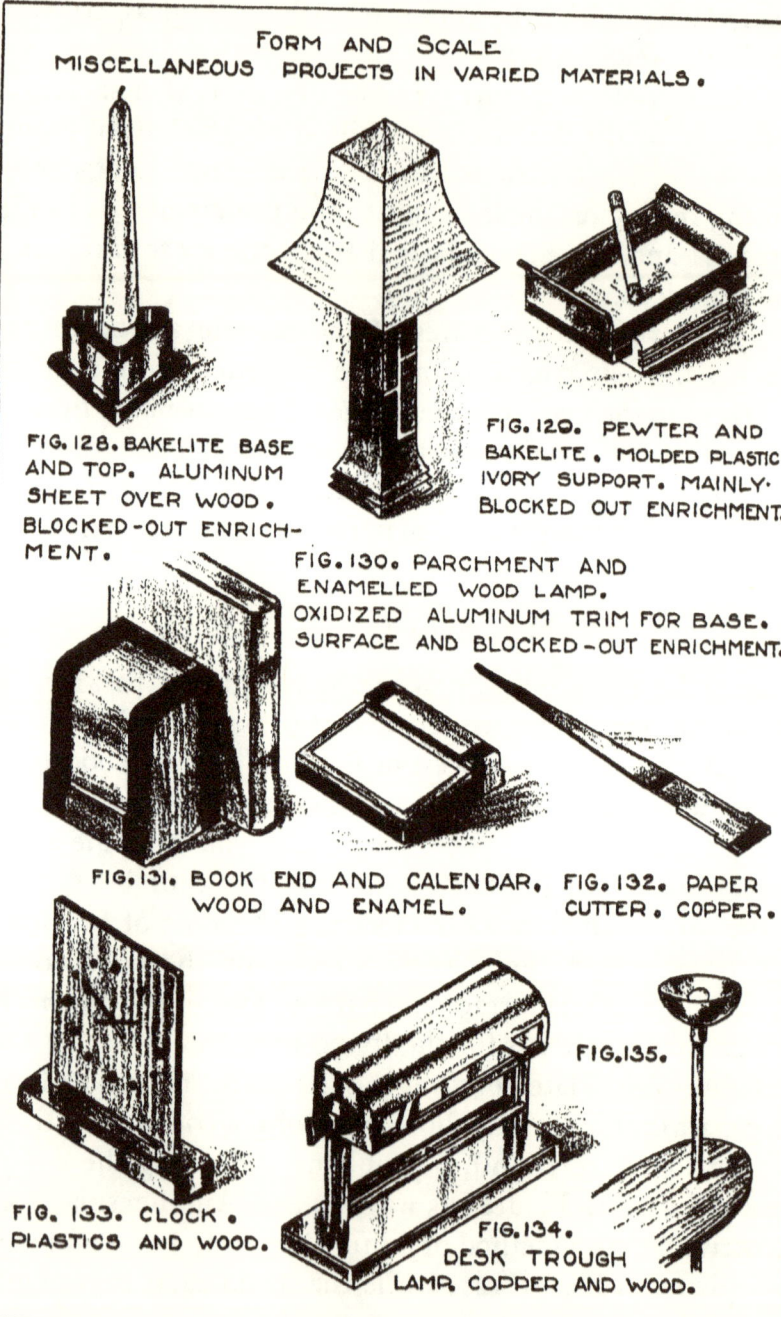

FORM AND SCALE
MISCELLANEOUS PROJECTS IN VARIED MATERIALS.

FIG.128. BAKELITE BASE AND TOP. ALUMINUM SHEET OVER WOOD. BLOCKED-OUT ENRICHMENT.

FIG.129. PEWTER AND BAKELITE. MOLDED PLASTIC IVORY SUPPORT. MAINLY-BLOCKED OUT ENRICHMENT.

FIG.130. PARCHMENT AND ENAMELLED WOOD LAMP. OXIDIZED ALUMINUM TRIM FOR BASE. SURFACE AND BLOCKED-OUT ENRICHMENT.

FIG.131. BOOK END AND CALENDAR. WOOD AND ENAMEL.

FIG.132. PAPER CUTTER. COPPER.

FIG.133. CLOCK. PLASTICS AND WOOD.

FIG.134. DESK TROUGH LAMP. COPPER AND WOOD.

FIG.135.

Plate 17

struction in bent wood. As shown, the cushion has been removed. New forms such as this are evolved by new uses of
material; they are far removed from the traditional, and
supply the motives for creative effort. As you will note, the
arm curves of Figure 125 must be in subtle relationship to
the horizontal motive of which they are a part.

Bent wood and a metal cross brace form the supports for
the table of Figure 126, Plate 16. An enameled wood top
gives the glitter and gayness latent in this design, while a
small, sharp groove with a strip of color enriches the whole
pattern. The usual treatment of the bent wood strip is to
leave it in its natural color, but the texture must be pleasing
and free from splinters.

Contour Enrichment

In his book on *Industrial Arts Design* the author placed
major emphasis on contour enrichment for the traditional
furniture considered in that book, particularly William and
Mary or Queen Anne, which were strongly emphatic in their
contours. In contemporary art, contour design, at least to a
great extent, has been supplanted by proportionate beauty
and surface or plastic enrichment. There seems, however, to
be a gradual trend towards *more emphasis on the contours*
as a means of enriching form; and, in bent wood furniture,
the bending process brings added emphasis on contours,
especially noticeable at turning or bending points. In metal
furniture, the bends likewise add a contribution to contour
emphasis; in fact, metal tubes *are* the contours.

For both bent wood and metal, the same contoural principle is applied. If possible, never use arcs of circles in contours and never make a bend exactly in the center of a mass
or a space division. Try for subtlety of curvature and use
your design ability in starting and terminating your bends
to give as much variety as is possible under structural conditions. Again, try to make your curves sweep with the major

thrust of the volume, or the space within the volume containing the curve; otherwise, design principles advanced within this book apply equally to curves of the contoural or outline types. Plates 14, 15, 16, have examples of contour enrichment, the direct outgrowth of materials and processes of construction. All metal and bent wood furniture must have one or more prominent masses to give contour construction the feeling of permanence and solidity.

MISCELLANEOUS PROJECTS

Plate 17 illustrates materials grouped into interesting combinations, in the spirit of the modern. The candlestick of Figure 128, Plate 17, with its plastic, shallow enrichment of receding planes has a trig smartness, as does the lamp of Figure 130. Plastics are becoming available for craftsmen and may be shaped in various ways, an example being the base for the pewter ash container of Figure 129.

Figures 131 and 132 present simple and similar problems for beginners. The copper paper cutter of Figure 132 may be oxidized, with the oxide removed at the points indicated. Figure 133 indicates modern trends in clocks. A small, discarded alarm clock is used for operating the hands, although a new set of works is preferable.

The tilting desk lamp of Figure 134 is illuminated by a tubular bulb readily purchased at most supply houses. Figure 135 is an indicator of the tendency towards indirect lighting to be located on the end of a desk or table.

All designs should first be planned within a well-considered volumetric casing and developed by modified isometric, as specified for wood design.

.

CHAPTER ELEVEN
ADVANCED PROBLEMS: UNIT PLANNING AND COLOR

A̲T this point, the reader is familiar with the major design problems of contemporary furniture, with current and anticipated uses. As systematic planning along geometric lines is regarded with favor by many designers, a problem of this type is herein illustrated, based on the possibilities latent in the 1.618 rectangle of the Hambidge Series of rectangles.

RHYTHM

The functional element of this problem is the demand for a low table, popular for its accessibility to chairs grouped around it and for its capacity for holding a number of articles varying in size. Then too, the stand is functional on three of its four sides with compartments or shelves entering the volume from three directions, leading to a more serviceable article.

Compare this stand with high, bulky pieces of furniture often found in small apartments where every inch of space counts, and you will find that low stands, by giving more overhead space, often relieve the room of a stuffy, filled-up feeling generated by too much mass and too little space.

Rhythm, the design principle entering into the spirit of this problem, is the feeling of aesthetic satisfaction, of pleasure experienced in seeing a number of objects or forms, arranged in such a manner as to cause our *attention* (rather than our eyes) to move smoothly, rhythmically over their pathway. The rhythmic lines of the dance drama, of draperies and human figures moving in unison. marching bodies of men: all are attention appeals to our rhythmic sensitivity. Our response may be so slight as to be unnoticeable, or we may move hands or some part of the body in response, even using the tactile approach and moving the fingers lightly along some long, flowing, rhythmic line.

As in all art principles, we dislike monotony and wherever possible avoid mechanical regularity in our rhythms. The exact spacings of a picket fence have little appeal compared with the rhythmic spacings of the step or set-back pattern. In one, we have monotony; in the other, variety.

This attention movement necessary for the perception of movement in rhythmic sequences becomes the theme for systematic design planning, using as a basis the whirling-square plan of procedure. The XM or 1.618 plus rectangle is now familiar to us and, in Figure 136, Plate 18, the rectangle has in the auxiliary plan been drawn to scale in modified isometric, indicated by the letters *A B C D* with the dimensions conveniently indicated in millimeters, projected from the line of measure.

Within this modified isometric rectangle, study the subdivisions marked by isometric squares, later to become masses and spaces; note how they whirl around rhythmically, getting smaller and smaller. This swirling pattern gives the XM rectangle the additional name of the whirling square. Steps generating this pattern are as follow:

1. To construct these squares, mark off to the left from point *A*, 50 mm.; project to the isometric view and draw *E F*, which is the first square to be planned.

2. Draw the diagonal *D B;* this cuts the side of the square *E F* at point *G;* draw *G G'*, which completes the second square. The area *F C B E* is a whirling square exactly similar in ratio to *A B C D*.

3. Draw the diagonal of *C F E B*, giving the line *E C*. This cuts the line *G G'* at *H*. Complete *H H'*, and the third square

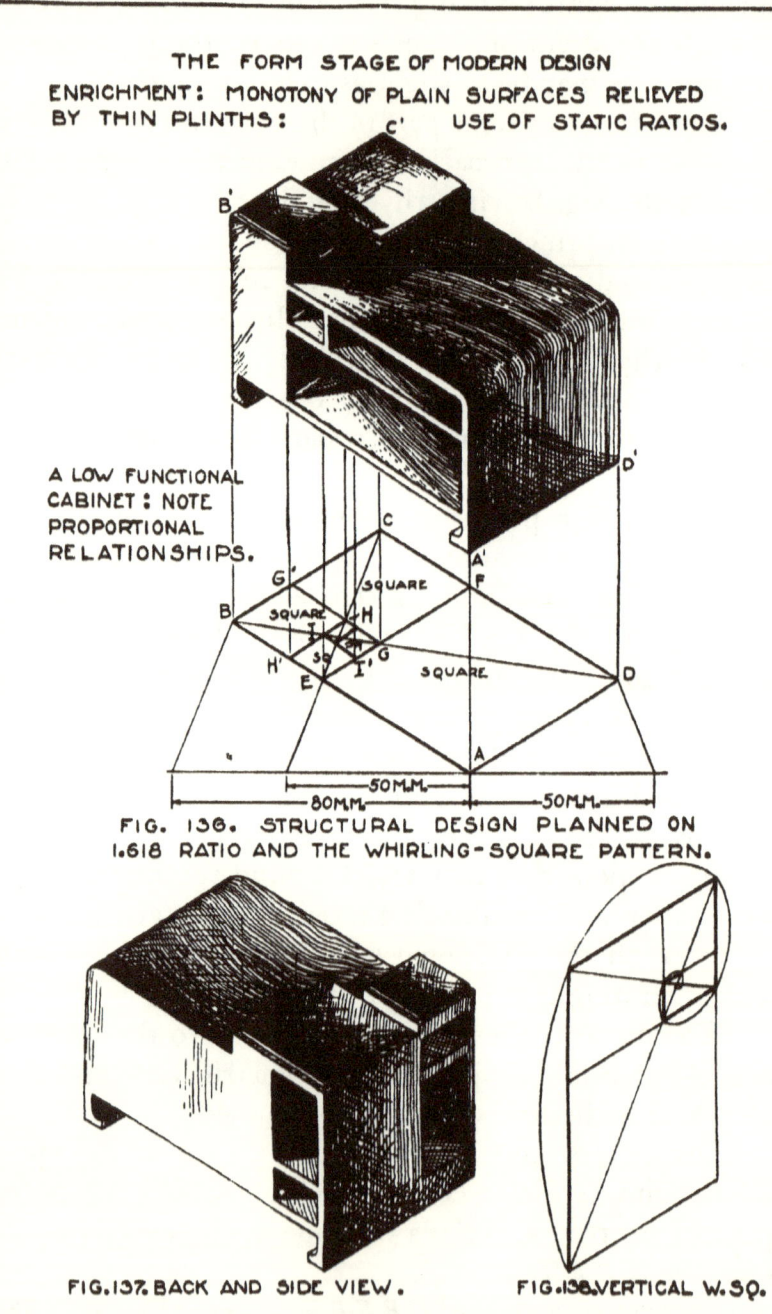

THE FORM STAGE OF MODERN DESIGN
ENRICHMENT: MONOTONY OF PLAIN SURFACES RELIEVED
BY THIN PLINTHS: USE OF STATIC RATIOS.

A LOW FUNCTIONAL
CABINET: NOTE
PROPORTIONAL
RELATIONSHIPS.

FIG. 136. STRUCTURAL DESIGN PLANNED ON
1.618 RATIO AND THE WHIRLING-SQUARE PATTERN.

FIG.137. BACK AND SIDE VIEW.

FIG.138.VERTICAL W.SQ.

Plate 18

is thus formed; while *G' G E B* form a whirling square similar to the two previously formed areas.

4. Where *H H'* cuts the diagonal *B D*, we have point *I*. By drawing *I I'*, the fourth square is created; and, where *I I'* cuts *E C*, we have a point locating the fifth square. This process can be continued theoretically forever. The squares would continue to whirl around the point termed the pole (the intersection of *B D C E*) but would never reach a point. It is an appeal to your imagination, but mathematically possible. For practical purposes, five squares are sufficient.

5. According to the requirements of the problem and in keeping with proportionate relationships, create an isometric volumetric casing. Then, projecting upward from the auxiliary isometric plan, as at points *A' B' C' D'*, complete the volume, the mass-and-space divisions, and then add the thickness which develops the form, using judgment tempered by specific requirements as to heights. The rhythmic action of the squares will now be observed, particularly in Figure 137. The project may be of gum wood or veneered, with the grain pattern running in the direction of the major thrusts.

This is an interesting problem: A static area like the square may be given a dynamic patterning, particularly when used within a strongly dynamic volume. The rectangle *A B C D* may be used in a number of ways; for example, *C F E B, B G' G E, E H' H G, I I' H G* are possible points for upward projection rather than the whirling squares.

Figure 138, the whirling-square rectangle in a vertical position, within its boundaries has a series of whirling squares exactly similar in plan to Figure 136. With the corners of the squares as points for the curve, a spiral has been drawn, with the distances between points bearing ratios of 1.618 to the preceding and succeeding points, and also the summation series of 3, 5, 8, 13, etc. The spiral constructed on this ratio is one of nature's curves, found in shells, fern fronds, and in a variety of growths. The curve, with its subtlety and variety, is considered the most beautiful of all curves, both in nature and in art; while the problem points out this ratio as one of nature's own proportions.

PSYCHOLOGICAL ASPECTS

The advanced designer may utilize geometric devices similar to the problem just presented, but eventually he will depend upon his own creative, unaided efforts. To aid him in these creative efforts, from time to time, we have brought functionalism to our aid as a starting-off point. Let us develop this point a bit further: Not only must our design be functional, but it must put the *consumer* in a mental state, leading him intuitively to *feel* that the object will fulfill its allotted objective, its duty.

Just how to do this depends upon the sensitivity of the designer to *human reactions to desires;* for it is his duty to satisfy these desires. Some human desires are natural and some acquired, and there is too much difference of opinion for a clear-cut and definite listing. Desires of interest to the designer include *rest and comfort,* a response to an organic need. The adult behavior response to a desire for rest and comfort is to find a good place for repose and for sleep. Again, furniture affording rest and exhaling a mental feeling that a man is going to rest comfortably, would not give the same feeling to a woman. Thus on Plate 19, Figure 139, is the design for a chair completely masculine and made for the tired man who drops into it after a hard day's work. The chair makes him "think comfort," linking functionalism and psychology in accordance with modern design approach.

In this chair and without reaching for a table, the smoker has equipment within his grasp. He may have difficulty in arising from the chair, but that small discomfort is more than balanced by his vast enjoyment; he may extend his feet and experience complete relaxation from the trials of our complex life.

In Figure 140, Plate 19, he has a low bookcase which may be placed near the chair; while books for other members of the family are arranged on another side, thus leaving him undisturbed. If he so desires, a screen, designed in sympathy with both stand and chair is at his disposal, tending towards privacy.

The desire to *escape from danger* certainly is a plea for good, sound construction, a leading tenet of the contemporary designer and a valid argument for metal furniture. Although the use of glass might be open to objection, particularly in a household with children, shatter-proof glass would meet this objection.

Two interesting and conflicting desires are *the wish to conform with what others are doing* and *the desire to be different from others*. In both instances there is a desire to escape disapproval of others or a desire for approval. There is a tendency to conform to what leaders are doing and to be different from those we consider to be inferior. Styles are much concerned with the desire to conform, shown by the growth in the demand for modern types of furniture, while the desire to escape criticism will keep many from adopting the new and adhering to safe traditions. Another strong desire is to *explore the new*, regarding the experience as an adventure, as indeed did the author of this book—an adventure into a new field of thought. You, as participators, will experience this thrill of a new adventure into new processes and materials.

The *desire for play* is closely linked with the new leisure; the recreation room and the playground are prolific in suggestions for new problems. The *desire for cleanliness*, while very clear in many higher animals, seems divorced from human society as a basic instinct. Cleanliness then must be the result of training, with the desire to escape from disease playing its part, and, in the growing child, the desire to escape punishment, often the reward back of clean hands. Modern

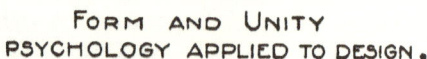

FORM AND UNITY
PSYCHOLOGY APPLIED TO DESIGN.

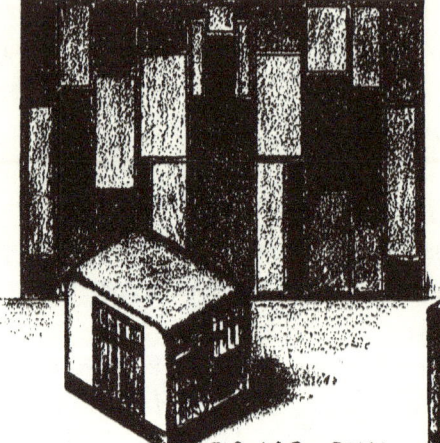

FIG. 140. DUAL
SERVICE CABINET
AND SCREEN.

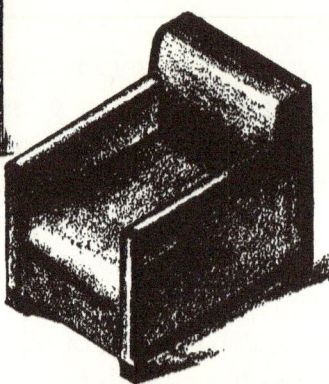

FIG. 139. PSYCHOLOGY OF
DESIGN-THINKING COMFORT:
LOW CHAIR • MASCULINE
CHARACTERISTICS.

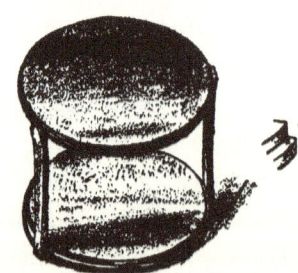

FIG. 141. LOW TABLE:
FEMININE CHARACTERISTICS.

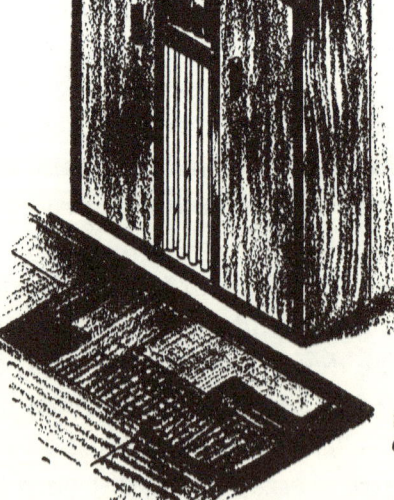

FIG. 142. BOOK CABINET WITH
OPEN SHELF FOR CURRENT
BOOKS.

Plate 19

furniture, simple and dustless, with its removable and easily cleaned cushions, ministers to the desire for a cleanliness far superior to the dust-catching and often elaborate period furniture.

The *desire for beauty* has much influence in shaping human action and may be rated high as a factor in life, varying, of course, with different groups on varying social levels. The class of society in which we move has an effect on the *desire for economy;* but it can be said that modern furniture on a factory basis is moderately priced and may be made at small outlay, depending upon the materials used. The strong appeal of the modern style is its marked functionalism, its ability to do the job or several jobs well; surely an appeal to the economically minded person.

Clearly the results of environment and education, the *desire to be hospitable* is illustrated in Figure 141, Plate 19, in which the coffee table, also serving for a light lunch table or flowers, is gracious and welcoming in its curves, light and easily portable, and distinctly feminine in appearance.

The desire for cleanliness is linked with order. Frequently we find scattered in disorder four or five current books in which we are interested, possibly from the lending library or book club. It may be that school books are with this collection, books which are needed for hurried exits to school or for a few moments of reading. The general bookcase is hardly a feasible place for them; neither is the cluttered table. Why not make a separate compartment in the bookcase for current or used books, and thus emphasize system and order? A bookcase of this type is shown in Figure 142, Plate 19, with the closed and dustproof cabinet for less used books.

UNIT PLANNING

For closing this chapter, there have been reserved two desires which deal with our contacts with others—*the desire to be with other people similar to ourselves* and *to be alone.*

The tired man or woman who drops into the chair frequently desires to be alone for rest and comfort, but there are times when the normal adult likes to foregather with others for talk or recreation.

For complete functioning of the desire for sociability, the modern living room is planned with its traffic lanes and parking places in which groups may be conveniently assembled for various purposes, and individual areas for the desire to be alone.

To gain space for these purposes, particularly in small apartments, and to increase the harmony of the modern room, it is customary to place the furniture parallel to the walls, with parking places made by assembling appropriate pieces still parallel to the walls. Figure 143, Plate 20, illustrates a suggested correct placing for modern styles, while Figure 144 on the same plate is the result of disorderly planning. Note the individual and group units in Figure 143.

To further orderly planning, designers are rapidly introducing what is known as the "unit system," whereby several pieces of furniture may be used as separate units or joined together quickly as a single unit. The chairs of Figure 143 may be used either singly or together.

Furthermore, many articles of furniture have the same height and depth but vary in widths. Thus, in Figure 143, the units against the rear wall may be a bookcase and a radio cabinet; assembled, they give the impression of one piece or unit; separated they may be grouped with other and similar pieces, as possibly a desk and a radio.

The advantages of this unit-assembling plan rest in the fact that it is possible to accentuate the major room thrust, to save space, and to establish order. In Figure 143, the major thrust is controlled by the rear wall, eighteen feet long. Two powerful, horizontal lines—the assembled radio and bookcase unit, and the lines of the couch unit—accentuate this thrust, establish thrust harmony, and make the room appear longer.

Space is gained, as is readily seen by studying Figure 144; while actually less furniture is used than in Figure 143, it seems more crowded. Order always gives more space than disorder. Where are the traffic lanes and parking places of Figure 144? Does not Figure 144 give the impression more of a number of people desiring to be alone, than of groups in social intercourse?

With the unit plan in operation, the scale of various articles in the room is brought into closer harmony. By making common denominators of heights and widths or depths of articles which may be grouped together, the volumetric casings are in better proportionate relation to each other. If one tires of one combination or grouping, readily and harmoniously another grouping or unit may be established. Thus sideboards, serving tables, men's dressers, women's dressers, bookcases, radios, desks are amenable to this treatment. By selecting a group of objects which go together, and by giving them common denominators of heights and depths, the inventive designer has at his command infinite change. In the units, he has strong, horizontal masses for room composition, space savers, and a logical simplification of the room equipment. It is only through modern design that the unit plan is possible; traditional furniture with its varied proportions is not capable of adjustments such as we have described.

COLOR

Without color plates, to describe the uses of modern color is difficult, and so the following suggestions may be regarded as guides rather than as complete methods of procedure.

Contrasted with the delicate, anemic colors of the past, modern color is clear and clean, and has more strength than formerly. Black is popular but, if used alone, as vitrolite, as

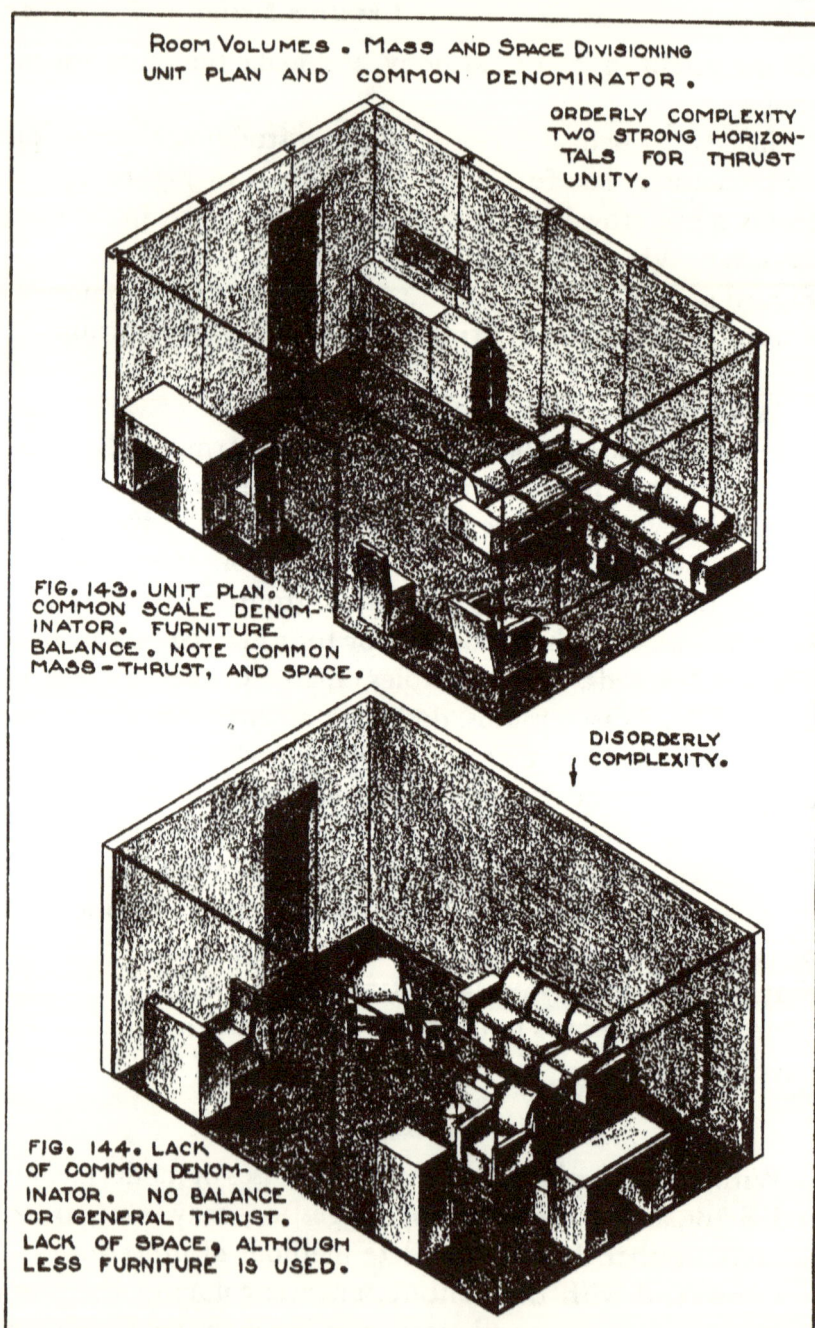

ROOM VOLUMES . MASS AND SPACE DIVISIONING
UNIT PLAN AND COMMON DENOMINATOR .

ORDERLY COMPLEXITY
TWO STRONG HORIZON-
TALS FOR THRUST
UNITY.

FIG. 143. UNIT PLAN.
COMMON SCALE DENOM-
INATOR. FURNITURE
BALANCE. NOTE COMMON
MASS-THRUST, AND SPACE.

DISORDERLY
COMPLEXITY.

FIG. 144. LACK
OF COMMON DENOM-
INATOR. NO BALANCE
OR GENERAL THRUST.
LACK OF SPACE, ALTHOUGH
LESS FURNITURE IS USED.

Plate 20

a plastic, or enamel, or lacquer, it has a depressing effect. Black bands as accents often are the making of a piece of furniture. Black with white is startling but may be used by the skillful designer. As a background, black develops the brilliancy of colors placed in front of it. Black and the silvery gleam of metal, as gray (a tint of black), is interesting; while a silvery mirror frame, simulated by metals, is considered more in keeping than the former gold mirror frames of historic periods.

A large area of white should not be used with small areas of other colors; but, in small quantities, white is harmonious with other colors. Paul Frankl, in his book, *New Dimensions,* gives the following colors which match well:

Red—white, yellow brown, orange
Orange—white, red, brown, yellow
Yellow—white, brown
Green—white, yellow, red, blue, brown, black
Blue—white, black
Purple—white, red, blue, black
Gray—all colors, including white
Black—all colors but not white

Oranges and yellows should be darkened a perceptible amount by adding gray; purple and blue should be lightened by adding a small amount of white. In other words, the oranges and yellows should be darkened toward a middle tone between white and black, and the blue and purple lightened toward the middle tone.

It is inadvisable to use equal areas of two colors: make one color control the scheme and use the other for accent. Small narrow bands of color are effective in full brilliancy.

Artists are agreed on the advancing and receding impressions received from looking at color; that is, some colors seem to come forward, others to go back. The cool colors, blue and purple, give the impression of depth; while the warm colors, yellow and orange, advance, with red and green maintaining a sort of middle distance between their warm and cool associates.

We can then avail ourselves of these relations to develop plastic enrichment. Paint the sunken or lower planes with receding color and the salient with advancing, while the intermediate planes may be in much-grayed red or green.

It is suggested that beginners use color with reserve and experiment with small projects like book ends. Small touches of color act as brilliant jewels in a room and are essential to its vitality; but colorful veneers, the reflections in glass and metal, bring color to the design often without further additions in pigmentary applications.

CHAPTER TWELVE
CREATIVE DESIGN

A HUMAN DESIRE PROJECT

IN this chapter, a method of creative design approach is presented which will be valid, regardless of changing styles or periods—a method based first on *human desires* and second on *functionalism,* two immovable factors beyond dispute. Moreover, the method suggested leaves the designer free to use his creative skill in the development of new forms and new construction based purely on the question of service and beauty.

The first step is to find a piece of furniture for which there is an actual and pressing need, based on an innate desire for its services. The field for this problem is, we shall say, in the room for a young man. His actions in dressing are observed. He appears to be in a hurry; he rummages quickly through his dresser drawer for a shirt which, with others, has been placed in an orderly pile, but with socks and other articles of wearing apparel. Shortly the desired shirt is selected, together with his socks, but the drawer has been completely upset. The same condition is encountered in the drawer containing collars and neckties, while a missing collar button makes of this drawer a turmoil of ties, collars, and handkerchiefs.

The young man departs in an ill-tempered rush, leaving a trail of untidiness, observing that he wishes he could dress and "keep things straight." Here is the case of a man basically trained to order and neatness, who likes cleanliness and his clean clothes in order. Let us see what modern creative design can do for him.

This young man likes style, a certain smartness in his furniture, and desires to be different. At the start of the problem, it is essential to make separate compartments for individual articles—shirts, neckties, soft collars, handkerchiefs, collar buttons, and dress studs; there are other articles which we might include, but these are illustrative of the method employed.

The space occupied by one-half dozen of each article enumerated is measured with some room to spare. The man feels that one-half dozen is about all he cares to consider, although more collars and handkerchiefs are to be desired.

These five spaces are visualized as volumes and are found, drawn to the scale of one-half inch to the foot, in Figure 145, Plate 21. Put together but without order, they are assembled in Figure 146 on the same plate.

These are the functional elements of the design; now comes the skill of the designer. Looking for some common denominators (as four inches in this case) or heights in common, we begin assembling the volumes into an integrated whole. The first assembly in Figure 147, Plate 21, is displeasing and lacking in integrated unity and rhythm; in other words, the units do not hold together.

And so another attempt produces Figure 148; but still this is unsatisfactory, although the effort is not wasted, for the assembled volumes suggest a progressive series of setbacks recalling Figure 136. With this idea as a basis, Figure 149 shows the final plan with the volumes separated for the wood construction—the form stage of development. In assembling these volumes, feel free to add slight amounts to the volumes for compactness, integration, and good proportioning. An example of this procedure is seen in Figure 148. In assembling the single volumes, it was noted that monotony existed in the space divisions; some of the masses were too nearly similar in size; it then became necessary to increase the minor volume for the neckties. This does not

FUNCTIONAL SPACE DESIGNING.

CREATIVE DESIGN BASED ON SPACE VOLUMES
FOR YOUNG MEN.

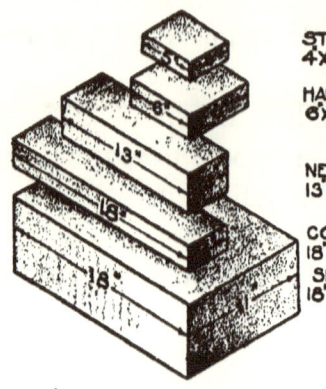

STUDS.
4 X 5 X 1½"

HANDK'S.
6 X 6 X 2"

NECKTIES.
13 X 4 X 3"

COLLARS.
18" X 4 X 4"
SHIRTS.
18" X 6" X 11"

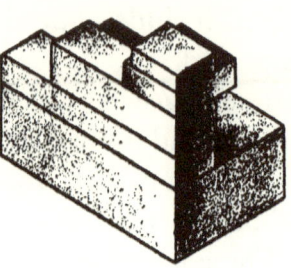

FIG. 146. VOLUMES
MASSED WITHOUT ORDER.

FIG. 145. VOLUMES, EACH CONTAINING
SIX ARTICLES OF ONE OR MORE SETS.

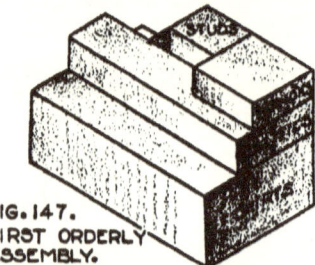

FIG. 147.
FIRST ORDERLY
ASSEMBLY.

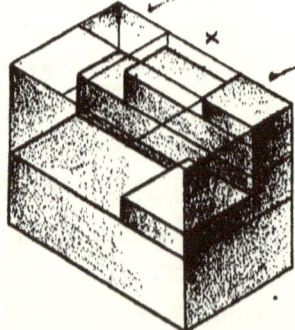

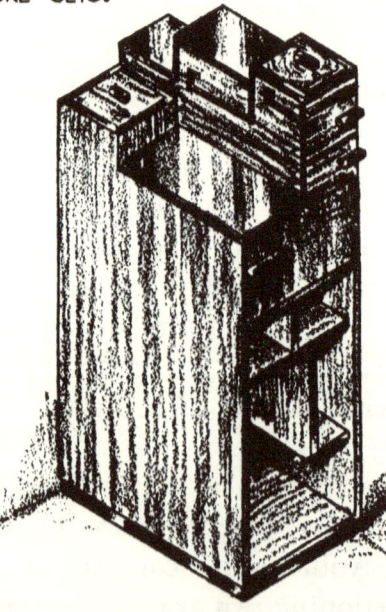

FIG. 148. SECOND ASSEMBLY.
NOTE PROPORTIONATE CHECKS
WITHIN VOLUMETRIC CASING.

FIG. 149. THIRD ASSEMBLY.
AND FORM STAGE COM-
PLETED WITH CONSTRUCTION.
FINAL PROPORTIONATE PATTERN.

Plate 21

disturb the function of that space, for neckties vary in lengths and usually are folded once.

The volume of the minor parts now becomes a minor volume of the whole design or of the major volume of which the correct and convenient height has to be ascertained. As the major volume assumes shape, the mind should be kept open to all impressions of a creative nature. Possibilities of additional shelving in the lower portions of the volume may be included as a part of the pattern and closed by doors or left open. These arrangements will give the plastic character to the volume; but as the article is intended for a young man, it should have a masculine appearance, be extremely durable and, of course, simple and thus in keeping with modernism.

Regarding construction and materials, let us put hinged covers on the stud and handkerchief boxes while the other articles are placed in drawer containers. On examining several dressers, holes made by cigarette burns noted lapses from the neatness supposedly innate in this man, giving ample reason for using some form of fireproof plastic on surfaces exposed to this danger.

In Figure 149, the problem stands complete, a crystallization of orderly functionalism arising in human desires, and a lucid exposition of the modern method of attack. While the motive primarily is vertical, that is, the volumetric casing is vertical in character and is so supported by shelving, the top minor masses have a horizontal thrust. The thrust problem, then, is one of balancing the contrasting tendencies; and, for this purpose, appendages and enrichment are called into play, introducing at the same time an element of smartness and style, of interest to the man. Metal or ebony inlay will give durability and sparkle to the design.

This method of approach is applicable to many problems involving human needs. Check common articles of furniture —do they bring functionalism and beauty into daily life?

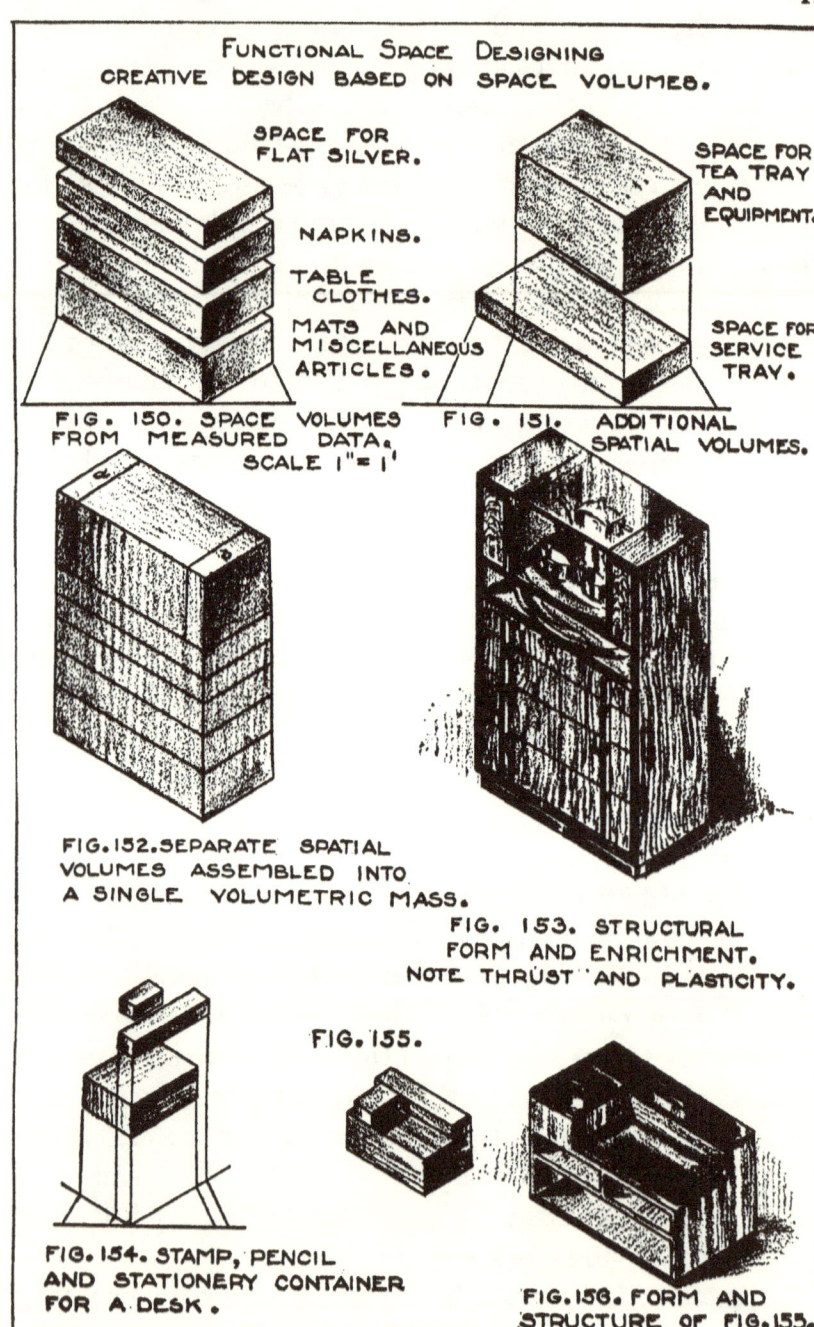

FUNCTIONAL SPACE DESIGNING
CREATIVE DESIGN BASED ON SPACE VOLUMES.

SPACE FOR
FLAT SILVER.

SPACE FOR
TEA TRAY
AND
EQUIPMENT.

NAPKINS.

TABLE
CLOTHES.

MATS AND
MISCELLANEOUS
ARTICLES.

SPACE FOR
SERVICE
TRAY.

FIG. 150. SPACE VOLUMES
FROM MEASURED DATA.
SCALE 1"= 1'

FIG. 151. ADDITIONAL
SPATIAL VOLUMES.

FIG. 152. SEPARATE SPATIAL
VOLUMES ASSEMBLED INTO
A SINGLE VOLUMETRIC MASS.

FIG. 153. STRUCTURAL
FORM AND ENRICHMENT.
NOTE THRUST AND PLASTICITY.

FIG. 155.

FIG. 154. STAMP, PENCIL
AND STATIONERY CONTAINER
FOR A DESK.

FIG. 156. FORM AND
STRUCTURE OF FIG. 155.

Plate 22

UTILITY CABINET FOR THE DINING ROOM

A combination chest of drawers and serving table has been developed by the method just described, and found detailed on Plate 22. The spaces desirable for flat silver, napkins, table cloths, mats, and miscellaneous articles were measured, recorded, and arranged according to size in Figure 150, Plate 22. As these were being measured, it was observed that the tea service and serving tray were placed on top of the existing chest with the serving tray tilted precariously against the wall.

The designer constantly is alert to possibilities of functional improvements, and thus the idea of including these items in the plan for the chest matured; their space volumes were measured as in Figure 151, Plate 22.

Assembled in an approach to rhythmic sequence, the combined minor volumes appear as a single volume in Figure 152, and represent in their combined totalities the actual functioning volume of the cabinet. To make an integrated volume of these minor volumes, two small spaces were added at *a* and *b*, Figure 152—added in such a manner as to make a symmetrical and balanced design of the whole. While in Plate 21, the widely divergent natures of the containers seemed to suggest asymmetrical patterning, the spaces of the present problem made symmetry advisable.

The question arises as to the disposition of added spaces like *a* and *b*, Figure 152. Some designers would prefer to turn these into compartments, but the chest seems sufficiently complex as it now stands and the decision is to make the added space nonfunctional—surely a small amount of wasted space in payment for the harmony added to the design.

Developing this problem to the form stage, we have Figure 153, Plate 22. With the pleasant gleam of silver in mind, the top is of plate glass through which the silver reflects its colors, while the glass top makes an excellent and clean serving table. Among other details, attention is directed to the use of drawer handles assembled in strips for unity and placed directly under divisions *a* and *b,* continuing their vertical thrusts.

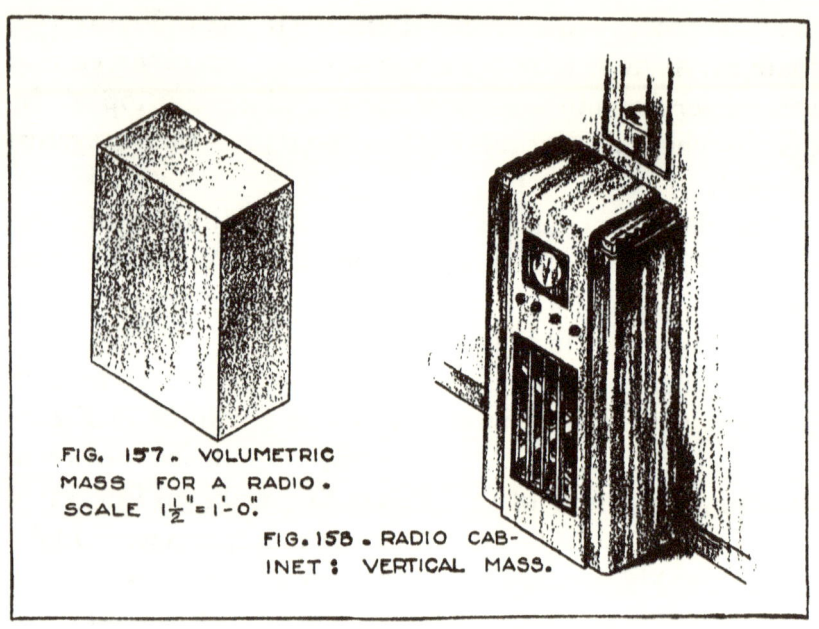

FIG. 157 . VOLUMETRIC MASS FOR A RADIO . SCALE $1\frac{1}{2}" = 1'-0"$.

FIG. 158 . RADIO CAB- INET : VERTICAL MASS.

MISCELLANEOUS PROBLEMS

A much simpler problem appears in Figure 154, Plate 22, assembled in Figure 155, and developed to the form stage in Figure 156. The design needs little explanation; the lower compartments are for envelopes and letter paper. If the beginner in design finds difficulty in assembling minor volumes, it is suggested that a number of wooden blocks be made to scale, each block representing a volume for some distinct purpose, as collars, silverware, and so on. Select the blocks desired for the problem and pile them in different arrangements until a pleasing composition results from your efforts. Indeed, a functional collection of volumes for all sorts of uses—a roller-skate volume, another for shoes, and one for baseballs—would make an interesting part of any classroom equipment. Let it be understood that there is nothing childish in this, as one of the great industrial design schools in Europe uses nonfunctioning blocks for proportionate study.

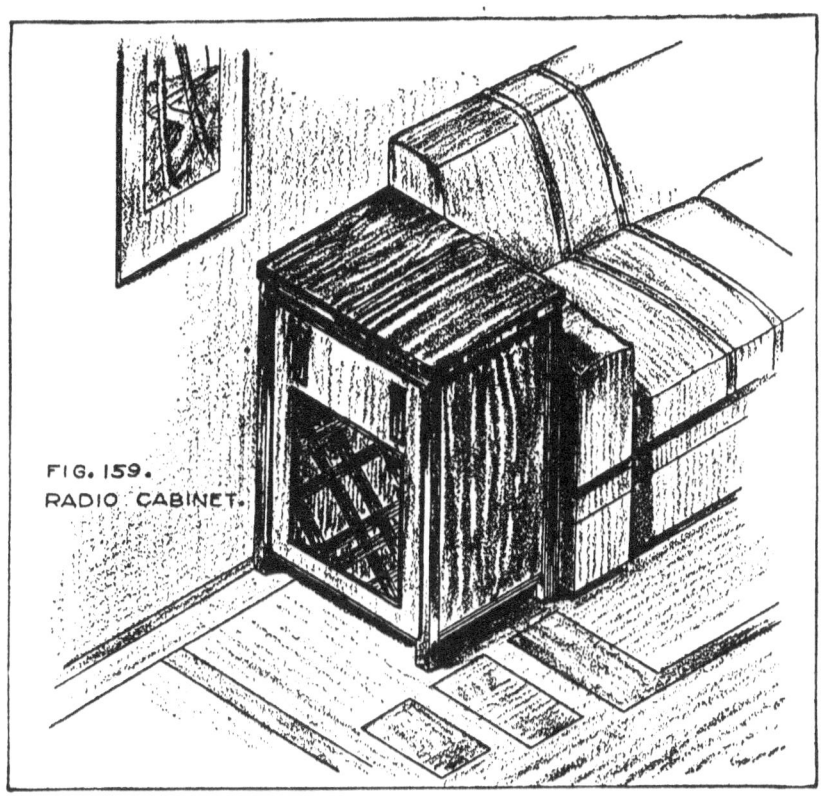

FIG. 159.
RADIO CABINET.

The volumetric mass for a radio, Figure 157, becomes the radio cabinet of Figure 158, with the diagonal tapestry weave symbolic of radio impulses. There is a growing demand for concealed radio dials, hidden under top covers—a demand worked out in Figures 159 from the data supplied by Figure 157. When it is desired, the occupant of the couch opens the lid of his cabinet and readily enough manipulates the dials. This infrequent radio user has an end table for general use, quickly formed by bringing the leaves together, thus making the radio cabinet function in a dual capacity.

Throughout this book we have directed the reader toward channels of good taste, toward the pleasure of creative expression, leading to the construction of objects saturated with service to society. Let the author leave with his reader three guardian words, three maxims for good modern design—BEAUTY, EFFICIENCY, and ECONOMY—interlocked and inseparable and without which no industrial product can exist.

DECIMAL EQUIVALENTS OF FRACTIONS OF AN INCH

Fraction	Decimal	Fraction	Decimal	Fraction	Decimal	Fraction	Decimal
1/64 =	.015625	17/64 =	.265625	33/64 =	.515625	49/64 =	.765625
1/32 =	.03125	9/32 =	.28125	17/32 =	.53125	25/32 =	.78125
3/64 =	.046875	19/64 =	.296875	35/64 =	.546875	51/64 =	.796875
1/16 =	.0625	5/16 =	.3125	9/16 =	.5625	13/16 =	.8125
5/64 =	.078125	21/64 =	.328125	37/64 =	.578125	53/64 =	.828125
3/32 =	.09375	11/32 =	.34375	19/32 =	.59375	27/32 =	.84375
7/64 =	.109375	23/64 =	.359375	39/64 =	.609375	55/64 =	.859375
1/8 =	.125	3/8 =	.375	5/8 =	.625	7/8 =	.875
9/64 =	.140625	25/64 =	.390625	41/64 =	.640625	57/64 =	.890625
5/32 =	.15625	13/32 =	.40625	21/32 =	.65625	29/32 =	.90625
11/64 =	.171875	27/64 =	.421875	43/64 =	.671875	59/64 =	.921875
3/16 =	.1875	7/16 =	.4375	11/16 =	.6875	15/16 =	.9375
13/64 =	.203125	29/64 =	.453125	45/64 =	.703125	61/64 =	.953125
7/32 =	.21875	15/32 =	.46875	23/32 =	.71875	31/32 =	.96875
15/64 =	.234375	31/64 =	.484375	47/64 =	.734375	63/64 =	.984375
1/4 =	.25	1/2 =	.5	3/4 =	.75	1 =	1.0

METRIC CONVERSIONS

Mm. to In.

Mm.	In.		Mm.	In.
1 =	.0394		17 =	.6693
2 =	.0787		18 =	.7087
3 =	.1181		19 =	.7480
4 =	.1575		20 =	.7874
5 =	.1968		21 =	.8268
6 =	.2362		22 =	.8661
7 =	.2756		23 =	.9055
8 =	.3150		24 =	.9449
9 =	.3543		25 =	.9843
10 =	.3937		26 =	1.0236
11 =	.4331		27 =	1.0630
12 =	.4724		28 =	1.1024
13 =	.5118		29 =	1.1417
14 =	.5512		30 =	1.1811
15 =	.5906		31 =	1.2205
16 =	.6299		32 =	1.2598

In. to Mm.

In.	Mm.		In.	Mm.
1/32 =	.79		17/32 =	13.49
1/16 =	1.58		9/16 =	14.28
3/32 =	2.38		19/32 =	15.08
1/8 =	3.17		5/8 =	15.87
5/32 =	3.96		21/32 =	16.66
3/16 =	4.76		11/16 =	17.46
7/32 =	5.55		23/32 =	18.25
1/4 =	6.34		3/4 =	19.04
9/32 =	7.14		25/32 =	19.84
5/16 =	7.93		13/16 =	20.63
11/32 =	8.73		27/32 =	21.43
3/8 =	9.52		7/8 =	22.22
13/32 =	10.31		29/32 =	23.01
7/16 =	11.11		15/16 =	23.81
15/32 =	11.90		31/32 =	24.60
1/2 =	12.69		1 =	25.39

INDEX